MEDIATIONS

ESSAYS ON RELIGIOUS PLURALISM
& THE PERENNIAL PHILOSOPHY

OTHER WORKS
BY HARRY OLDMEADOW

BOOKS

Traditionalism: Religion in the light of the Perennial Philosophy
Colombo: Sri Lanka Institute of Traditional Studies, 2000

Journeys East: 20th Century Western Encounters
with Eastern Religious Traditions
Bloomington: World Wisdom, 2004

A Christian Pilgrim in India:
The Spiritual Journey of Swami Abhishiktananda
Bloomington: World Wisdom, 2008

BOOKS EDITED

The Betrayal of Tradition:
Essays on the Spiritual Crisis of Modernity
Bloomington: World Wisdom, 2005

Light from the East: Eastern Wisdom for the Modern West
Bloomington: World Wisdom, 2007

MEDIATIONS

Essays on
Religious Pluralism
& the Perennial Philosophy

HARRY OLDMEADOW

SOPHIA PERENNIS

SAN RAFAEL, CA

First published in the USA
by Sophia Perennis
© Harry Oldmeadow 2008

Series editor: James R. Wetmore

For information, address:
Sophia Perennis, P.O. Box 151011
San Rafael, CA 94915
sophiaperennis.com

Library of Congress Cataloging-in-Publication Data

Oldmeadow, Harry, 1947–
Mediations: essays on religious pluralism and the
perennial philosophy / Harry Oldmeadow.— 1st ed.

p. cm.
Includes bibliographical references (p.).
ISBN 978-1-59731-082-6 (pbk: alk. paper)
1. Religious pluralism. 2. Tradition (Philosophy).
I. Title
BL 85.O43   2008
200—dc22   2008005660

CONTENTS

Introduction 1

René Guénon, Metaphysician 3

Ananda Coomaraswamy and Traditional Art 29

Rudolf Otto, the East, and Religious Inclusivism 44

C.G. Jung & Mircea Eliade: 'Priests without Surplices'? 64

Allen Ginsberg, A Buddhist Beat 94

Swami Abhishiktananda, Fr Jules Monchanin, and the
      Hindu-Christian Encounter 110

Frithjof Schuon, A Sage for the Times 132

Acknowledgments 153
The Perennial Philosophy: Recommended Reading 155
Note on the Author 158

Introduction

Some years ago Father Bede Griffiths remarked that 'the rediscovery of religion is the great intellectual, moral and spiritual
adventure of our time' (from *The Golden String*). To yield its full
treasure this rediscovery must entail a reaffirmation of the
perennial wisdom which has informed the world's mythological
and religious traditions since time immemorial but which has
been obscured and neglected in the West over the last five hundred years. The figures portrayed in the following essays have all
played a significant role in recovering the Wisdom of the Ages.

In the domain of religion and metaphysics the emergence of
the 'traditionalist' or 'perennialist' school has been one of the
most remarkable phenomena of the last century. Its pre-eminent exponents are René Guénon, Ananda Coomaraswamy, and
Frithjof Schuon. The perennialists have elucidated the metaphysical and cosmological principles which govern all integral
religious and sapiential traditions, and have explicated the manifold ways in which these principles are expressed in the particular and varied forms of different civilizations.

The work of the perennialists first came to my attention in
the mid-1970s. Since that time, and under their influence, I have
devoted myself to the study of the world's religious traditions.
Ananda Coomaraswamy, referring to the boundless realm of
Tradition, once observed that 'if you ever really enter this
world ... you may never again be contented with what you have
been accustomed to think of as "progress" and "civilization"....'
(from his essay 'Philosophy of Mediaeval Art'). And so it has
proved. But in the course of my explorations I have also encountered many arresting modern figures who do not belong within
the perennialist school and who thus, in various ways, are vulnerable to the confusions and follies of modernity. Nonetheless,
several of these thinkers have deepened and enriched our

understanding of religion, especially when their insights are assimilated into a traditional outlook.

The essays herein focus on the three great perennialists already mentioned—Guénon, Coomaraswamy, and Schuon—and on half a dozen other important thinkers and practitioners: Rudolf Otto, Mircea Eliade, Carl Jung, Allen Ginsberg, Fr Jules Monchanin, and Swami Abhishiktananda. Each of these individuals has, in different ways, confronted one of the decisive events of the modern era, the collision of differing religious traditions from all over the globe; each has been a mediator between the different spiritual worlds now everywhere impinging on each other. The resolution of the peculiar tensions and antagonisms arising out of this unprecedented global situation, and the fulfilment of its inherent spiritual possibilities, is one of the most urgent tasks facing all those concerned with the spiritual welfare of humanity. It is my hope that this modest collection, gathering together previously scattered writings, may play a small part in that noble task, and that it might be of interest to scholars of religion and spiritual wayfarers alike.

These pieces were written over a quarter century. I have resisted the temptation to revise and expand them, with the exception of the final essay on Frithjof Schuon which has been slightly enlarged. Whilst today I might sometimes express things differently I find little in these essays which I now want to disavow.

The spelling of foreign terms has been standardized throughout; such terms are invariably italicized. Full details are provided the first time a work is cited in a particular essay; thenceforth abbreviated titles are used.

I register my deep gratitude to Michael Fitzgerald and James Wetmore for their part in bringing this volume to fruition, and to my brother Peter who first kindled my interest in the spiritual universe of the East.

Harry Oldmeadow
Bendigo, Australia

René Guénon,
Metaphysician

*[T]here are those whose vocation it is to provide the keys with which
the treasury of wisdom of other traditions can be unlocked, revealing
to those who are destined to receive this wisdom the essential unity
and universality and at the same the formal diversity of tradition and
revelation.[1]*
                          Seyyed Hossein Nasr

A Biographical Sketch

It is remarkable that one of the 20th century's most formidable
writers on metaphysical and cosmological subjects should
remain so little known outside his native France and beyond
perennialist circles. The art historian and metaphysical expositor, Ananda Coomaraswamy, himself profoundly influenced by
Guénon's work, wrote of him:

> [T]he least important thing about Guénon is his personality
> or biography.... The fact is he has the invisibility that is
> proper to the complete philosopher....[2]

The American traditionalist, Whitall Perry, who knew Guénon
personally, speaks of his 'outer anonymity' and of this 'austere yet

---

1. S.H. Nasr, *Sufi Essays* (London: Allen & Unwin, 1972), p126.
2. Letter to Kurt Leidecker, November 1941, *Selected Letters of Ananda Coomaraswamy*, ed. R.P. Coomaraswamy and A. Moore, Jr, (New Delhi: Oxford, 1988),
pp49–50.

benevolent figure . . . ungraspable and remote.'[1] There is indeed
something elusive and enigmatic about René Guénon the man.
He left a formidable legacy of writings but his personal life
remains shrouded in obscurity. In France he has always
commanded a small but dedicated following and academic
interest in Guénon shows some sign of burgeoning there.
Elsewhere he remains a shadowy figure whose name occasionally
crops up in reference to French occultism or his pioneering study
(in the West) of Advaita Vedanta. The growing interest in Guénon
has generated no small amount of controversy amongst French
scholars about some aspects of his life, especially in the years from
1906 to 1912.[2] Here we shall confine ourselves to a biographical
sketch which leaves aside some of these unresolved questions and
includes only such material for which there appears to be
persuasive evidence and reputable authority.[3] Furthermore, we
shall focus on those aspects of his life which might shed light on
his work.

René Guénon was born in Blois in 1886. He grew up in a strict
Catholic environment and was schooled by Jesuits. As a young
man he moved to Paris to take up studies in mathematics at the
Collège Rollin. Maths remained a lifelong interest and a few
years before his death he published a short mathematical trea-
tise, *Les principes du calcul infinitésimal*. However, his energies were
soon diverted from academic studies and in 1905 he abandoned
his preparation for *Grandes Écoles*. For the next seven years, seized
by what Anatole France called 'the vertigo of the invisible',

1. W. Perry, 'Coomaraswamy: the Man, Myth and History', *Studies in Comparative Religion*, 11:3, 1977, p160, and 'The Man and the Witness' in *Ananda Coomaraswamy, Remembering and Remembering Again and Again*, ed. S.D.R. Singam ((Kuala
Lumpur: privately published, 1974), p6.

2. Some of these controversies have been dispassionately discussed in J.P.
Laurant, 'Le problème de René Guénon, ou Quelques questions posées par les
rapports de sa vie et de son oeuvre', *Revue de l'Histoire des religions*, 179:1, 1971,
pp41–70.

3. The only English-language biography, somewhat unsatisfactory, is Robin
Waterfield's *René Guénon and the Future of the West* (Hillsdale, NY: Sophia Perennis, 2002).

Guénon submerged himself in *fin-de-siècle* French occultism. He became a leading member in several secret societies—theosophical, spiritualistic, masonic and 'gnostic'.

Guénon's involvement in the occultist underground seems to have been somewhat indiscriminate. From the vantage-point of his later work it was a murky and bizarre period in his life, one of which he apparently did not care to be reminded. Nevertheless, Guénon learned a good deal in this period and indeed, he was eventually to become one of the most unsparing critics of these occultist movements. We will not here unravel the details of Guénon's participation in various secret societies. However, it is worth pausing to reflect on the significance of this period in his life. In its sociological dimension occultism provided, as doubtless it still does, a framework for the repudiation of the bourgeois ideologies and institutions of the day. Most of the occult groups turned to the archaic past in search of authentic spiritual values against which modern civilization was measured and found wanting. As Mircea Eliade has observed,

> involvement with the occult represented for the French literary and artistic avant-garde one of the most efficient criticisms and rejections of the religious and cultural values of the West—efficient because it was considered to be based on historical facts.[1]

Although Guénon was to disown the philosophical and historical assumptions on which such movements were built and to contrast their 'counterfeit spirituality' with what he came to see as authentic expressions of esotericism, he remained steadfastly opposed to contemporary European civilization.

Some of the occult movements stimulated a study of ancient esoteric traditions in Egypt, Persia, India, and China, and directed attention towards the sacred writings of the East. Precisely how Guénon came to a serious study of Taoism, Hinduism and Islam remains unclear but it seems likely that it was through

1. M. Eliade, *Occultism, Witchcraft and Cultural Fashions* (Chicago: University of Chicago, 1976), p53.

his involvement in one of the occultist groups. Whitall Perry has suggested that the 'catalyzing element' was Guénon's contact in Paris with some Indians of the Advaita school.[1] The facts of the matter are far from clear and there is insufficient evidence to make speculation fruitful. Guénon always kept a cloak of secrecy tightly wrapped around his own spiritual life. In June 1909, Guénon founded the occultist journal *La Gnose*, subtitled '*organe de l'Eglise gnostique universelle*'. It lasted a little over two years and carried most of his writings from this period which, although they exhibit some rationalistic and anti-religious bias, demonstrate a familiarity with Vedanta.

Guénon's life entered a new phase in 1912, one marked by his marriage to a devout Catholic. He emerged from the rather subterranean world of the occultists and now moved freely in an intensely Catholic milieu, leading a busy social and intellectual life. He was influenced by several prominent Catholic intellectuals of the day, among then Jacques Maritain, Fathers Peilleaube and Sertillanges, and one M. Milhaud, who conducted classes at the Sorbonne on the philosophy of science. The years 1912 to 1930 were the most public of Guénon's life. He attended lectures at the Sorbonne, wrote and published widely, gave public lectures himself, and maintained many social and intellectual contacts. He published his first books in the 1920s and soon became well known for his work on philosophical and metaphysical subjects.

Whatever Guénon's personal commitments may have been during this period his thought had clearly undergone a major shift away from occultism towards an interest in sapiential traditions within the framework of the great religions. One of the foci of interest for Guénon was the possibility of a Christian esotericism within the Catholic tradition. (He always remained somewhat ignorant of the esoteric dimensions of

---

1. W. Perry, 'The Revival of Interest in Tradition' in *The Unanimous Tradition*, ed. R. Fernando (Colombo: Sri Lanka Institute of Traditional Studies, 1991), pp8–9.

Eastern Orthodoxy.)[1] Olivier de Fremond, a friend of those years, wrote of Guénon's letters from this period, *'Les vieilles lettres que j'ai de lui respirent un parfait esprit catholique.*'[2] In some of his work in this period, Guénon envisaged a regenerated Catholicism, enriched and invigorated by a recovery of her esoteric traditions and 'repaired' through a *prise de conscience*.[3] He contributed regularly to the Catholic journal *Regnabit*, the Sacré-Coeur review founded and edited by P. Anizan. These articles reveal the re-orientation of Guénon's thinking in which 'tradition' now becomes the controlling theme. Some of these periodical writings found their way into his later books.

The years 1927 to 1930 mark another transition in Guénon's life, culminating in his move to Cairo in 1930 and his open commitment to Islam. A conflict between Anizan (whom Guénon supported) and the Archbishop of Rheims, and adverse Catholic criticism of his book *Le roi du monde* (1927),[4] compounded a growing disillusionment with the Church and hardened Guénon's suspicion that it had surrendered to the 'temporal and material'. In January 1928 Guénon's wife died rather abruptly. Following a series of fortuitous circumstances Guénon left on a three month visit to Cairo.[5] He was to remain there until his death in 1951.

In Cairo Guénon was initiated into the Sufi order of Shadilites and invested with the name Abdel Wahed Yahya. He married again and lived a modest and retiring existence:

1. Guénon's view of Christianity has been discussed in P.L. Reynolds *René Guénon: His Life and Work* (unpublished), p9ff. See also B. Kelly, 'Notes on the Light of the Eastern Religions' in *Religion of the Heart*, ed. S.H. Nasr & W. Stoddart (Oakton: Foundation for Traditional Studies, 1991), pp160–161.

2. Quoted in J.P. Laurant, 'Le problème...' p57. (Trans: 'These old letters I have from him breathe a perfect Catholic spirit.')

3. J.P. Laurant, 'Le problème...' pp57–59. See also R. Guénon, *Crisis of the Modern World* (Ghent: Sophia Perennis, 2004), chap. 7.

4. English translation: *The King of the World* (Hillsdale, NY: Sophia Perennis, 1999).

5. J.P. Laurant, 'Le problème...', p60.

such was his anonymity that an admirer of his writings was dumbfounded to discover that the venerable next door neighbor whom she had known for years as Sheikh Abdel Wahed Yahya was in reality René Guénon.[1]

A good deal of Guénon's energies were directed in the 1930s to a massive correspondence he carried on with his readers in Europe, often people in search of some kind of initiation, others simply pressing inquiries about subjects dealt with in Guénon's books and articles. Most of Guénon's published work after his move to Cairo appeared in *Études Traditionnelles* (until 1937 *Le Voile d'Isis*), a formerly theosophical journal which under Guénon's influence was transformed into the principal European forum for traditionalist thought. It was only the war which provided Guénon with enough respite from his correspondence to devote himself to the writing of some of his major works, including *The Reign of Quantity* (1945).

In his later years Guénon was preoccupied with questions concerning initiation into authentic esoteric traditions. He published at least twenty-five articles in *Études Traditionnelles* dealing with this subject from many different angles. Although he had found his own resting-place within the fold of Islam, Guénon remained interested in the possibility of genuine initiatic channels surviving within Christianity. He also never entirely relinquished his interest in Freemasonry and returned to this subject in some of his last writings. It was only shortly before his death that he concluded there was no effective hope of an esoteric regeneration within either masonry or Catholicism.

The relationship between Guénon's life and his work has engaged the attention of several scholars. Jean-Pierre Laurant has suggested that his intellectual, spiritual and ritual life only achieved a harmonious resolution after his move to Cairo and within the protective embrace of Islam.[2] P.L. Reynolds has charted the influence of his French and Catholic background

---

1. W. Perry, 'Coomaraswamy', p160.
2. J.P. Laurant, 'Le problème...', pp66–69.

on his work.[1] Others, especially those committed to traditionalism themselves, have argued that Guénon's whole adult life represents a witness to an unchanging vision of the truth and that
his participation in occultism was part of this function. Such
commentators suggest that his thought does not 'evolve' but
only shifts ground as Guénon responds to changing circumstances. Thus Michel Valsan, a collaborator on *Études Traditionnelles*, writes:

> Il convient de préciser en l'occurrence que le privilège spé-
> cial qu'a cette oeuvre de jouer le rôle de critère de vérité,
> de régularité et de plénitude traditionnelle devant la civili-
> sation occidentale dérive du caractère sacré et non-invi-
> duel qu'a revêtu la fonction de René Guénon. L'homme qui
> devait accomplir cette fonction fut certainement préparé
> de loin et non pas improvisé. Les matrices de la Sagesse
> avaient prédisposé et formé son entité selon une économie
> précise, et sa carrière s'accomplit dans le temps par une
> corrélation constante entre ses possibilités et les conditions
> cycliques extérieures.[2]

Each of these kinds of claims carries some weight. The shaping
influence of Guénon's own background and period is obvious
enough in his work. Nor is there any point in denying that,
looked at as a whole, Guénon's thought does undergo a radical
change between about 1910 and 1914. While much of his early
work remains interesting and often illuminating it cannot be

---

1. P.L. Reynolds, *René Guénon*. These influences, Reynolds argues, account
for various imbalances and inadvertencies in Guénon's work.

2. M. Valsan in the Special Issue of *Études Traditionnelles: Le Sort de l'Occident*,
Nov. 1951. (Trans: It is useful to clarify in the present case that the special privi-
lege of truth which belongs to this work of playing the role of truth, regularity
and traditional plenitude in the face of Western civilisation derives from the
sacred and non-individual character that clothed the function of René
Guénon. The man who had to accomplish this function would certainly have
been prepared from long ago rather than improvising [his role]. The matrices
of Wisdom had predisposed and formed his being according to a precise economy, and his career fulfilled itself in time by a constant correlation between
his possibilities and the exterior cyclic conditions [of the age].)

said to represent a strictly traditionalist view such as we find in his later works. Given Guénon's education and background he could not have come to a traditionalist understanding without passing through a period in which he would learn to shed some modernistic (which is to say, anti-traditional) views and assumptions. To borrow one of his own favorite images, his early work is not without fissures which left it vulnerable to some of the more fanciful theories of the occultists. However, if we leave aside a few jejune writings from these early years, Guénon's work does exhibit an arresting consistency, an intuitive grasp of metaphysical and cosmological principles and an authoritative explication of the *sophia perennis*. One commentator has observed that after the occultist period Guénon only revised his position on two substantial issues: the authenticity of Buddhism as an integral tradition and the initiatic possibilities of Freemasonry.[1] If we add to this his changing attitude to the revival of Christian esotericism we have indeed catalogued all the radical revisions in Guénon's work in almost forty years. We shall return to this aspect of Guénon's achievement in discussing his own perception of the role he had to play.

Guénon's Writings

Guénon was a prolific writer. He published seventeen books during his lifetime, and many posthumous collections and compilations have since appeared. Here we shall take an overview of his work. The *oeuvre* exhibits certain recurrent motifs and preoccupations and is, in a sense, all of a piece. Guénon's understanding of tradition is the key to his work. As early as 1909 we find Guénon writing of 'the Primordial Tradition which, in reality, is the same everywhere, regardless of the different shapes it

---

1. M. Bastriocchi, 'The Last Pillars of Wisdom' in *Ananda Coomaraswamy: Remembering and Remembering*, p359, n8. S.H. Nasr writes of the lack of 'development' in Guénon's work that it was 'as if he had written them all [his books] at one sitting and then published them over the next few decades'; *Knowledge and the Sacred* (New York: Crossroad, 1981), p101.

takes in order to be fit for every race and every historical period.'[1] As the English traditionalist, Gai Eaton, has observed, Guénon

> believes that there exists a Universal Tradition, revealed to humanity at the beginning of the present cycle of time, but partially lost...his primary concern is less with the detailed forms of this Tradition and the history of its decline than with its kernel, the pure and changeless knowledge which is still accessible to man through the channels provided by traditional doctrine....[2]

The existence of a Primordial Tradition embodying a set of immutable metaphysical and cosmological principles from which derive a succession of traditions each expressing these principles in forms determined by a given Revelation and by the exigencies of the particular situation, is axiomatic in Guénon's work.[3] It is a first principle which admits of no argument; nor does it require any kind of 'proof' or 'demonstration', historical or otherwise.

Guénon's work, from his earliest writings in 1909 onwards, can be seen as an attempt to give a new expression and application to the timeless principles which inform all traditional doctrines. In his writings he ranges over a vast terrain—Vedanta, the Chinese tradition, Christianity, Sufism, folklore and mythology from all over the world, the secret traditions of gnosticism, alchemy, the Kabbalah, and so on, always intent on excavating their underlying principles and showing them to be formal

---

1. R. Guénon, 'La Demiurge', *La Gnose*, 1909; quoted in M. Bastriocchi, 'The Last Pillars', p351. See R. Guénon, *Miscellania* (Hillsdale, NY: Sophia Perennis, 2003), chap. 1.

2. Gai Eaton, *The Richest Vein* (Hillsdale, NY: Sophia Perennis, 2005), pp188–189.

3. The relationship between the Primordial Tradition and the various traditions needs clarification in that while each tradition in fact derives its overall form and principal characteristics from a particular Revelation, it nevertheless carries over (in many of its aspects) certain essential features of the tradition which precedes it.

manifestations of the one Primordial Tradition. Certain key themes run through all of his writings and one meets again and again with such notions as these: the concept of metaphysics transcending all other doctrinal orders; the identification of metaphysics and the 'formalization', so to speak, of gnosis (or *jñana* if one prefers); the distinction between the exoteric and esoteric domains; the hierarchic superiority and infallibility of intellective knowledge; the contrast of the modern Occident with the traditional Orient; the spiritual bankruptcy of modern European civilisation; a cyclical view of Time, based largely on the Hindu doctrine of cosmic cycles and, as a corollary, a contra-evolutionary view of history. Guénon gathered together doctrines and principles from diverse times and places but emphasized that the enterprise was a synthetic one which envisaged formally divergent elements in their principial unity rather than a syncretic one which press-ganged incongruous forms into an artificial unity. This distinction is a crucial one not only in Guénon's work but in traditionalism as a whole.[1]

Guénon repeatedly turned to oriental wisdoms, believing that it was only in the East that various sapiential traditions remained more or less intact. Advaita Vedanta provided the bedrock of Guénon's own metaphysical expositions. It is important not to confuse this stance with the kind of sentimental exoticism nowadays so much in vogue. As Coomaraswamy noted,

> If Guénon wants the West to turn to Eastern metaphysics, it is not because they are Eastern but because this is metaphysics. If 'Eastern' metaphysics differed from a 'Western' metaphysics—one or the other would not be metaphysics.[2]

One of Guénon's translators made the same point in suggesting that if Guénon turns so often to the East it is because the West is in the position of the

---

1. See R. Guénon, *The Symbolism of the Cross* (Hillsdale, NY: Sophia Perennis, 2004), preface, and *Crisis of the Modern World*, preface and chap. 9.
2. A. Coomaraswamy, *The Bugbear of Literacy* (London: Perennial Books, 1979), pp 72–73.

foolish virgins who, through the wandering of their attention in other directions, had allowed their lamps to go out; in order to rekindle the sacred fire, which in its essence is always the same wherever it may be burning, they must have recourse to the lamps still kept alight.[1]

The contrast between the riches of traditional civilizations and the spiritual impoverishment of modern Europe sounds like a refrain through Guénon's writings. In all his work

Guénon's mission was twofold: to reveal the metaphysical roots of the 'crisis of the modern world' and to explain the ideas behind the authentic and esoteric teachings that still remained alive . . . in the East.[2]

By way of an expedient we can divide Guénon's writings into five categories, each corresponding roughly with a particular period in his life: the occultist periodical writings of the pre-1912 period; the reaction against and critique of occultism, especially spiritualism and theosophy; writings on Oriental metaphysics; on aspects of the European tradition and on initiation; and, fifthly, the critique of modern civilisation. Guénon's earliest writings appeared, as we have seen, in the organs of French occultism. In the light of his later work some of this periodical literature must be considered somewhat ephemeral. Nonetheless the seeds of most of Guénon's work can be found in articles from this period. The most significant, perhaps, were five essays which appeared in *La Gnose* between September 1911 and February 1912, under the title '*La constitution de l'être humain et son évolution selon le Védânta*'; these became the opening chapters of one of his most influential studies, *Man and His Becoming According to the Vedanta*, not published until 1925. Other writings from this period on such subjects as mathematics and the science of numbers, prayer, incantation, and initiation, all presage later work.

---

1. Quoted in G. Eaton, *The Richest Vein*, p199.
2. Jacob Needleman in his Foreword to *The Sword of Gnosis*, ed. J. Needleman (Baltimore: Penguin, 1974), pp11–12.

The shift in Guénon's intellectual orientation away from occultism is difficult to pinpoint. However, as early as 1909 we find him attacking what he saw as the misconceptions and confusions abroad in the spiritualist movements.[1] Whilst his misgivings about many of the occultist groups were growing in the 1909-1912 period it was not until the publication of two of his earliest books that he mounted a full-scale critique: *Le théosophisme, histoire d'une pseudo religion* (1921) and *L'erreur spirite* (1923). The titles are suggestive: these were lacerating attacks not only on theosophy and spiritualism but also on the 'gnostic' groups founded by a certain Dr. Encausse (who achieved some celebrity as 'Papus'), and on movements such as Rosicrucianism. Guénon's exposé was not merely a polemical fusillade but a meticulously detailed analysis. Of the groups in which Guénon himself had been involved only the Masons escaped relatively unscathed. As Eliade has noted,

> The most erudite and devastating critique of all these so-called occult groups was presented not by a rationalist outside observer, but by an author from the inner circle, duly initiated into some of their secret orders and well acquainted with their occult doctrines; furthermore, that critique was directed, not from a sceptical or positivistic perspective, but from what he called 'traditional esotericism'. This learned and intransigent critic was René Guénon.[2]

The details of this demolition job need not concern us here but it is worth noting the main lines of Guénon's attack. The most fundamental part of Guénon's indictment was that such movements, far from preserving traditional esotericisms, were made up of a syncretic mish-mash of distorted and heteroge-

---

1. R. Guénon, 'La Gnose et les Ecoles Spiritualistes', *La Gnose*, Dec. 1909. See also P. Charconac, 'La vie simple de René Guénon' in the Special Issue of *Études Traditionnelles*, November 1951, p321 (English translation: *The Simple Life of René Guénon* [Ghent: Sophia Perennis, 2001]).
2. M. Eliade, *Occultism*, p51.

neous elements forced into a false unity, devoid of any authentic metaphysical framework. Thus they were vulnerable to the scientistic ideologies of the day and inevitably fell prey to the intellectual confusions rampant in Europe. One of the most characteristic confusions of such groups, to cite but one example, was the mistaking of the psychic for the spiritual. Occultism as a whole he now saw as one of the 'signs of the times', a symptom of the spiritual malaise in modern civilisation. Guénon took up some of these charges again in later works, especially *The Reign of Quantity.*

Guénon's interest in Eastern metaphysical traditions had been awakened some time around 1909 and some of his early articles in *La Gnose* are devoted to Vedantic metaphysics. His first book, *Introduction générale à l'étude des doctrines hindoues* (1921) marked Guénon as a commentator of rare authority. It also served notice of Guénon's role as a redoubtable critic of contemporary civilisation. Of this book Seyyed Hossein Nasr has written,

> It was like a sudden burst of lightning, an abrupt intrusion into the modern world of a body of knowledge and a perspective utterly alien to the prevalent climate and world view and completely opposed to all that characterizes the modern mentality.[1]

However, Guénon's axial work on Vedanta, *L'homme et son devenir selon le Védânta*, was published in 1925. Other significant works in the field of oriental traditions include *La métaphysique orientale*, delivered as a lecture at the Sorbonne in 1925 but not published until 1939, *La Grande Triade*, an explication of traditional Chinese metaphysics and cosmology, and many articles on such subjects as Hindu mythology, Taoism and Confucianism, and reincarnation. Interestingly, Guénon remained more or less ignorant of the Buddhist tradition for many years, regarding it as no more than a 'heterodox development' within Hinduism and without integrity as a formal religious tradition.

---

1. S.H. Nasr, *Knowledge and the Sacred*, p101.

It was only through the intervention of Ananda Coomaraswamy and Marco Pallis, one of his translators, that Guénon revised his attitude to Buddhism.[1]

During the 1920s when Guénon was moving in the coteries of French Catholicism he turned his attention to some aspects of Europe's spiritual heritage. As well as numerous articles on such subjects as the Druids, the Grail, Christian symbolism and folkloric motifs, Guénon produced several important works in this field, including *L'esotérisme de Dante* (1925), *St Bernard* (1929), and *Le symbolisme de la croix* (1931). Another work, *Autorité spirituelle et pouvoir temporel* (1929), was occasioned by certain contemporary controversies. A collection of Guénon's masterly writings on symbolism has recently appeared in English translation for the first time under the title *Symbols of Sacred Science* (2001). However, the quintessential Guénon is to be found in two works which tied together some of his central themes: *La crise du monde moderne* (1927) and his masterpiece, *Le règne de la quantité et les signes des temps* (1945). The themes of these two books had been rehearsed in an earlier work, *Orient et Occident* (1924). Each of these books mounted an increasingly elaborate and merciless attack on the foundations of the contemporary European worldview. Let us turn to the last of these works.

The Reign of Quantity is a magisterial summation of Guénon's work. It is, characteristically, a difficult work. He was quite unconcerned with reaching a wide audience and addressed the book to those few capable of understanding it 'without any concern for the inevitable incomprehension of the others.'[2] He set out to challenge nearly all of the intellectual assumptions current in Europe at the time. The book, he writes, is directed to

---

1. This change in Guénon's attitude has been documented and discussed by several commentators, including Marco Pallis in 'A Fateful Meeting of Minds: A.K. Coomaraswamy and René Guénon', *Studies in Comparative Religion*, 12:3–4, 1978, pp180–181.

2. R. Guénon, *The Reign of Quantity & the Signs of the Times* (Hillsdale, NY: Sophia Perennis, 2004), p4.

the understanding of some of the darkest enigmas of the modern world, enigmas which the world itself denies because it is incapable of perceiving them although it carries them within itself, and because this denial is an indispensable condition for the maintenance of the special mentality whereby it exists.[1]

At first sight the book ranges over a bewildering variety of subjects: the nature of time, space and matter as conceived in traditional and modern science; the philosophical foundations of such typically modern modes of thought as rationalism, materialism and empiricism; the significance of ancient crafts such as metallurgy; the nature of shamanism and sorcery; the 'illusion of statistics'; the 'misdeeds of psychoanalysis'; the 'pseudo-initiatic' pretensions of spiritualism, theosophy and other 'counterfeit' forms of spirituality; tradition and anti-tradition; the unfolding of cosmic and terrestrial cycles. Some study of the book reveals that these apparently disparate strands have been woven into a work of subtle design and dense texture. *The Reign of Quantity* is a brilliantly sustained and excoriating attack on modern civilisation. It has less polemical heat and moral indignation than some of his earlier works but is none the less effective for that. The book is a controlled and dispassionate but devastating razing of the assumptions and values of modern science. At the same time it is an affirmation of the metaphysical and cosmological principles given expression in traditional cultures and religions.

Guénon unfolds a startling thesis, in the light of the doctrine of cosmic cycles, about the present terrestrial situation. His vision is rooted in the Hindu conception of the *Kali-Yuga* but is not restricted to the purely Indian expression of this doctrine. There is a dark apocalyptic strain in the book which some readers are tempted to dismiss as the rantings of another doom-sayer. For Guénon the dire circumstances in which the modern world finds itself are largely to be explained through an elucidation of

1. R. Guénon, *The Reign of Quantity*, p4.

the cyclic doctrine whereby humankind is seen to be degenerating into an increasingly solidified and materialized state, more and more impervious to spiritual influences. Inversely, the world becomes increasingly susceptible to infernal forces of various kinds.[1] The forced convergence of different civilizations is the spatial correlate of the temporal unfolding of the present terrestrial cycle, moving towards an inexorable cataclysm.

Guénon took the inevitable end of the world absolutely seriously.[2] By the time of writing this book he believed there were no possible 'remedies', no escape from the apocalypse. To some readers this looks like a 'despairing pessimism' to which Guénon might have retorted that neither optimism nor pessimism had anything to do with the case. Moreover, what from one angle might be seen as a 'worldly pessimism', appears from another as a 'celestial optimism' since the end of a cycle marks its completion and the restoration of a true order.

Closely related to the doctrine of cycles is Guénon's profoundly challenging thesis about the nature of time, space and matter, one based on traditional cosmologies. Contrary to the claims of modern science, says Guénon, time and space do not constitute a kind of uniform continuum in the matrix of which events and material phenomena manifest themselves. Rather, time-and-space is a field of *qualitative* determinations and differences. In other words, the nature of time and space is not a constant, fixed datum but is subject to both quantitative and qualitative change. Any exclusively quantitative and materialistic science such as now tyrannizes the European mind cannot accommodate this principle. It strives rather to reduce qualitatively determined phenomena to the barren and mechanistic formulae of a profane and materialistic science. (One might add that some of the so-called 'discoveries' of physicists since

1. Herein, from the traditionalist viewpoint, lies the explanation for the modern excrescence of what Christopher Evans has called 'cults of unreason' —scientology, UFO-ism, Lobsang Rampa-ism, and so on. See C. Evans, *Cults of Unreason* (London: Harrap, 1973).

2. See J.P. Laurant, 'Le problème...', p58.

Guénon's time have done nothing to disprove his thesis and indeed, to some minds, give it more credibility. Guénon himself would have argued that metaphysical and cosmological principles such as he was applying could in no way be affected by empirical considerations.)[1]

Guénon's critique of scientism—the ideology of modern science—is much more than just another attack on scientific reductionism, although that surely is part of his case. Nor is it a catalogue of the inadequacies of this or that scientific theory. Rather, it is a radical and disturbing challenge to almost every postulate of modern European science. The critique hinges on the contrast between sacred, traditional sciences on the one hand, and a profane, materialistic science on the other. In an earlier work Guénon had elaborated the basis of this contrast in uncompromising terms:

> Never until the present epoch had the study of the sensible world been regarded as self-sufficient; never would the science of this ephemeral and changing multiplicity have been judged truly worthy of the name of knowledge.... According to the ancient conception...a science was less esteemed for itself than for the degree in which it expressed after its own fashion...a reflection of the higher immutable truth of which everything of any reality necessarily partakes...all science appeared as an extension of the traditional doctrine itself, as one of its applications, secondary and contingent no doubt...but still a veritable knowledge none the less....[2]

For Guénon, the notion of a self-sufficient, self-validating, autonomous material science is a contradiction, an incongruity,

---

1. For some discussion of the 'fissures' in modern science see Titus Burckhardt, *Mirror of the Intellect* (Cambridge: Quinta Essentia, 1987) and Wolfgang Smith, *Cosmos and Transcendence* (San Rafael, CA: Sophia Perennis, 2008).

2. This passage is quoted in Gai Eaton, *The Richest Vein*, p196. The source is not given but for a more extended discussion of precisely this contrast see Guénon's *Crisis of the Modern World*, chap. 4.

for all sciences must have recourse to higher and immutable principles and truths. Science must be pursued in a metaphysical and cosmological framework which it cannot construct out of itself. In another work Guénon wrote that modern science,

> in disavowing the principles [of traditional metaphysics and cosmology] and in refusing to re-attach itself to them, robs itself both of the highest guarantee and the surest direction it could have; there is no longer anything valid in it except knowledge of details, and as soon as it seeks to rise one degree higher, it becomes dubious and vacillating.[1]

These principles, of course, are quite alien to the modern mentality. They are likely to provoke all kinds of quite irrelevant responses about the material inadequacies of traditional cosmologies.

The Reign of Quantity also seeks to demonstrate the intimate connections between traditional metaphysics and the arts, crafts, and sciences which are found in any traditional culture, and to show how many modern and profane sciences are really a kind of degenerated caricature of traditional sciences.[2] Such a demonstration turns largely on Guénon's explanation of the nature of symbolism and of the initiatic character of many traditional sciences.

Guénon's Role
and the Reception of His Work

What of the qualities of mind and temperament revealed in Guénon's writings? Marco Pallis wrote of

> a mind of phenomenal lucidity of a kind one can best describe as 'mathematical' in its apparent detachment from anything savoring of aesthetic or even moral considerations;

---

1. Quoted in W.T. Chan, 'The Unity of East and West', in *Radhakrishnan: Comparative Studies in Philosophy Presented in Honour of His Sixtieth Birthday*, ed. W.R. Inge, et. al., (London: Allen & Unwin, 1951), pp107–108.
    2. See R. Guénon, *The Reign of Quantity*, p6.

his criteria of what was right and what was inadmissible remained wholly intellectual ones needing no considerations drawn from a different order of reality to reinforce them—their own self-evidence sufficed.[1]

Another commentator speaks of Guénon's exposition as 'so crystalline and geometric, so mathematically abstract and devoid of almost any human element,'[2] while Gai Eaton notes that 'in him the blade of French intellectuality is tempered to a razor-sharp edge.'[3] Theodore Roszak writes of his 'keen, spiritual discrimination,'[4] while Frithjof Schuon, referring to the absence of any sentimental or even psychic dimension in Guénon's work, once used the image of 'an eye without a body.'[5] These images of sharpness, of a finely-honed cutting edge, a mathematical precision and incisive penetration, all testify to Guénon's clarity of thought in his metaphysical expositions and his pitiless exposure of the 'signs of the times'. Nonetheless, Guénon's work is by no means easy to assimilate. Gai Eaton, despite his admiration of Guénon, concedes that 'It is questionable whether anyone with the normal tastes and intellectual background of our day can approach Guénon's work for the first time without a sense of revulsion.'[6] Why so?

Firstly there is the substance of Guénon's work. It is not easy of access and, at first sight, often strange, startling, baffling. His premises are too radically at odds with conventional wisdom for him to gain any easy following. His critique of European civilisation is so ruthless, so unnerving in its implications, that it often provokes a kind of defensive reflex, an emotional and

---

1. M. Pallis, 'A Fateful Meeting of Minds', p178. The word 'intellectual' in this passage does not mean 'mental' but refers to the intellect as understood in medieval scholasticism, the faculty of transcendent realization, of gnosis.

2. W. Perry, 'Coomaraswamy', p163. See also W. Perry, 'The Revival of Interest in Tradition', p11.

3. G. Eaton, *The Richest Vein*, p184.

4. T. Roszak, *Unfinished Animal* (New York: Harper & Row, 1977), p15.

5. Quoted in W. Perry, 'Coomaraswamy', p163.

6. G. Eaton, *The Richest Vein*, p184.

intellectual resistance which makes for a failure to engage with what is actually being said. Without the right kind of predisposition the reader is unlikely to recover from the initial shock. An acceptance of Guénon's general thesis also entails a drastic intellectual and existential adjustment which few readers are willing to make. André Gide typified this kind of response to Guénon's work when he wrote,

> If only I had known Guénon is my youth!... Now it is too late; the die is cast. My sclerosed mind has as much diffi-culty conforming to the precepts of that ancestral wisdom as my body has to the so-called 'comfortable' position rec-ommended by the Yogis.... To tell the truth, I cannot even manage really to desire resorption of the individual into the Eternal Being they seek.... I cling desperately to my limits and feel a repugnance for the disappearance of those contours that my whole education made a point of defining.... I am and remain on the side of Descartes and of Bacon. None the less, those books of Guénon are remarkable....[1]

This is very much to the point. Guénon's vision cannot be accepted 'a little'. One might, of course, disagree over details but his fundamental premises must be either accepted or rejected. There is nothing of the *smörgåsbord* in Guénon's writings.

Then, also, there is Guénon's claim to being a mouthpiece for a metaphysical vision or *theoria* which is beyond the reach of 'proof', even of debate. Take for instance, the following:

> Those who are qualified to speak in the name of a tradi-tional doctrine are not required to enter into discussion with the 'profane' or to engage in polemics: it is for them simply to expound the doctrine such as it is, for the sake of those capable of understanding it, and at the same time to denounce error wherever it arises... their function is not

1. A. Gide, *The Journals of André Gide*, vol. 4, 1939–1949 (London: Secker & War-burg, 1951), p226.

to engage in strife and in doing so to compromise the doctrine, but to pronounce the judgement which they have the right to pronounce if they are in effective possession of the principles which should inspire them infallibly.[1]

Such a passage is likely, to say the least, to stick in the craw of many contemporary scholars for reasons obvious enough. For Guénon a genuine understanding of metaphysical principles represented a 'permanent and changeless certitude' which left no room for debate: one either understood these principles or one did not. Guénon was not bent on 'proving' anything whatsoever, only on making traditional doctrines more intelligible.

Hand in hand with this perception of his role went a tone of implacable certitude, all too easily seen as a kind of intellectual arrogance. Roszak, for example, speaks of 'a mind whose very precision led to an aristocratic intolerance and an elitism that risked sterility.'[2] Roger Lipsey refers to Guénon's 'formidably intolerant'[3] attitude to the modern West while Pallis writes of his 'habitually hectoring tone...adopted in regard to people whose views he disapproved of.'[4] Bernard Kelly refers to the 'withering, intransigent, unbending' tone of Guénon's writings.[5] Jacques Lacarrière has regretted Guénon's 'aristocratism, his exclusive attachment to esoterism, his arbitrary rejection—and at times indeed, his faulty knowledge—of contemporary philosophies, plus his ferocious intellectualism.'[6]

There is in Guénon's work an adamantine quality, an austerity and inflexibility, and a combative tone as well as his 'icy brilliance.'[7] He was not one to coax, cajole or seduce his readers. He

1. R. Guénon, *Crisis of the Modern World*, p67.

2. T. Roszak, *Unfinished Animal*, p15.

3. R. Lipsey, *Coomaraswamy: Life and Work* (Princeton: Princeton University, 1977), p273.

4. M. Pallis, Letter to the Editor, *Studies in Comparative Religion*, 1:1, 1967, pp47–48.

5. B. Kelly, 'Notes on the Light of Eastern Religions', p160.

6. J. Lacarrière, *The Gnostics* (London: Peter Owen, 1977), p126.

7. G. Eaton, *The Richest Vein*, p183.

wrote as a man convinced he was in possession of timeless truths and he will brook no compromises. There is no concession to alternative points of view, no sense of a dialogue with his readers, no hospitality to any ideas at odds with those he is expressing. Something of Guénon's unyielding posture is evinced in the following passage (remember that he is writing in the 1920s):

> hitherto, so far as we are aware, no one else beside ourselves has consistently expounded authentic Oriental ideas in the West; and we have done so . . . without the slightest wish to propagandize or to popularize, and exclusively for the benefit of those who are able to understand the doctrines just as they stand, and not after they have been denatured on the plea of making them more readily acceptable....[1]

In an unusually personal vein he reprimanded a critic who had suggested that Guénon had 'passed' from Hinduism to Islam:

> We have never 'passed' from one thing to another, as all our writings abundantly prove; and we have no need to 'seek the truth' since we know (and we must insist upon this word) that it exists equally in all traditions....[2]

Doubtless, for many contemporaries such claims smack of extravagant confidence. However, the crucial point is this: to be offended by Guénon's 'arrogance' and to invalidate his message are two quite different matters. It is to the latter purpose that Guénon's would-be critics ought to address themselves. One should also perhaps add that in these times of a full-scale relativism any claim to certitude is likely to be dismissed, without any further consideration, as 'fanaticism' or some such. Looked at from another angle Guénon's militant posture is nothing other than an expression of his fierce commitment to the truth and it

---

1. R. Guénon, *Crisis of the Modern World*, p103.
2. Quoted in G. Eaton, *The Richest Vein*, p185.

is precisely his refusal to compromise first principles which
gives his work its power and integrity.[1]

Another factor helps to explain Guénon's comparative obscurity in the West: his methodology and his attitude to scholarship. We have already seen how, for Guénon, metaphysical
principles were self-evident and self-authenticating. This poses a
problem for the scholarly mind. However, the problem runs
deeper. If it were simply a matter of Guénon working from the
basis of certain clearly-stated premises there would be no more
reason to reject his work than that of many a philosopher or
theologian. No, the fact is that Guénon was, in Whitall Perry's
words, 'somewhat slipshod in scholarship':

> his certitude about principles lent a false sense of security
> on the factual level, where a little research would have suf-
> ficed to protect him from the barbs of orientalists who, if
> incognizant of metaphysical and spiritual truths, had at
> least done their homework.[2]

Guénon was never primarily a scholar. Father Sylvain Lévi, to
whom Guénon submitted a draft of *Introduction générale* as a possible doctoral thesis, recommended its rejection on the grounds
that

> Il entend exclure tous les éléments qui ne correspondent
> pas à sa conception ... tout est dans le Vedanta ... il fait bon
> marché de l'histoire et de la critique historique ... il est
> tout prêt à croire á une transmission mystique d'une vérité
> première apparue au génie humain dès les premiers âges du
> monde.... [3]

---

1. See I.R. Tucker, Letter to the Editor, *Studies in Comparative Religion*, 1:3, 1967,
pp141–144. (It was precisely Guénon's refusal to make concessions which
Coomaraswamy much admired. See Letter to Paul Furfey, undated, *Selected Letters*, p158.)

2. W. Perry, 'Coomaraswamy', p160.

3. Quoted in J.P. Laurant, 'Le problème...', p43. (Translation: He intentionally
excludes all the elements which do not correspond to his conception ... all is

This is not unjust. However, while Guénon can reasonably be reproached with a failure to 'do his homework' on the empirical and historical level, we must remember that he was a metaphysician concerned with first principles. If his application of these principles to contingent phenomena sometimes left room for a more scrupulous scholarship then this is indeed regrettable but it leaves the principles themselves quite unaffected.[1] This is sometimes forgotten by those who wish to force Guénon into the mould of the historian, the sociologist, the anthropologist, or the comparative religionist.

Guénon was quite out of sympathy with the prevailing ideals of academic scholarship. Nothing could have been further removed from the spirit of his work than the notion of scholarship for its own sake. 'Passion for research,' he said, 'taken as an end in itself is mental restlessness without end and without issue.'[2] As Roger Lipsey remarked, Guénon kept his distance from the academic intelligentsia: 'he mistrusted the academic mind and received abundant mistrust in return.'[3]

All of these factors conspired to limit Guénon's appeal. However, while his influence remains fairly minimal in the Western academic community at large, he is *the* seminal influence in the development of traditionalism, or, to use American terminology, perennialism. Along with Coomaraswamy and Schuon he forms what one commentator has called 'the great triumvirate' of the traditionalist school.[4] By way of concluding this introduction to Guénon we shall briefly consider

---

in the Vedanta ... he lightly dismisses history and historical criticism ... he is entirely ready to believe in a mystical transmission of a primordial truth which appeared to humanity in the earliest ages of the world.)

1. Furthermore, as Schuon has pointed out, 'one may have an intuition for pure principles without having one for a given phenomenal order, that is to say, without being able to apply the principles spontaneously in such and such a domain'; F. Schuon, *Sufism: Veil and Quintessence* (Bloomington: World Wisdom, 1980), p128.

2. From 'Orient et Occident', quoted in W. Perry (ed), *A Treasury of Traditional Wisdom* (London: Allen & Unwin, 1971), p732.

3. R. Lipsey, *Coomaraswamy*, p272.

4. E.J. Sharpe *Comparative Religion* (London: Duckworth,1975), p265.

his own perception of his role and the way in which he is seen by other perennialists.

For those who accept Guénon's premises his work is a voice in the wilderness of modernity. However, as both Schuon and Perry have stressed, Guénon's function cannot strictly be termed 'prophetic', the age of prophecy being over. Schuon:

> If on the doctrinal plane the Guénonian work has a stamp of unicity, it may not be useless to point out that this is owing not to a more or less 'prophetic' nature—a supposition that is excluded and which Guénon had already rejected beforehand—but to an exceptional cyclical conjuncture whose temporal aspect is this 'end of the world' in which we live, and whose spatial aspect is—by the same token—the forced convergence of civilizations.[1]

We have already met with Michel Valsan's contention to the same effect. Guénon himself did not doubt that he had access to the *sophia perennis* about which he wrote. In a conversation with Dr. Grangier in 1927 Guénon spoke of the wisdom to which he gave expression as '*impersonelle, d'origine divine, transmise par révélation, détachée et sans passion.*'[2] Although certain of his own intellectual realization of the truth Guénon never assumed the role of the spiritual master; he consistently refused those who requested initiation from him.[3]

Like other traditionalists, Guénon did not perceive his work as any kind of essay in creativity or personal 'originality', repeatedly emphasising that in the metaphysical domain there was no room for 'individualist considerations' of any kind. In a letter to a friend he wrote, 'I have no other merit than to have expressed

---

1. From F. Schuon, 'L'Oeuvre', in W. Perry, 'Coomaraswamy', p160. For further reflections see F. Schuon, *René Guénon: Some Observations* (Hillsdale, NY: Sophia Perennis, 2004).

2. From T. Grangier, *Souvenirs sur René Guénon*, quoted by J.P. Laurant, 'Le problème...', p58.

3. See J.P. Laurant, 'Le problème...', pp62–64. On the term 'spiritual master' see F. Schuon, 'Nature and Function of the Spiritual Master', *Studies in Comparative Religion*, 1:2, 1967, pp50–59.

to the best of my ability some traditional ideas.'[1] When reminded of the people who had been profoundly influenced by his writings he calmly replied, 'such disposition becomes a homage rendered to the doctrine expressed by us in a way which is totally independent of any individualistic consideration....'[2] Like Coomaraswamy, Guénon, certainly did not see himself building a new philosophy or creating a new school of thought. If it is sometimes necessary to speak of the traditionalist 'school' this is merely an expedient. For the traditionalists Guénon is the 'providential interpreter of this age.'[3] 'It was his role to remind a forgetful world, "in a way that can be ignored but not refuted", of first principles and to restore a lost sense of the Absolute.'[4]

1. W. Perry, 'The Man and His Witness', p7.
2. M. Bastriocchi, 'The Last Pillars', p356.
3. F. Schuon, 'L'Oeuvre', quoted by M. Bastriocchi, 'The Last Pillars', 359.
4. W. Perry, 'Coomaraswamy', 163.

Ananda
Coomaraswamy
and Traditional Art

*He was one of the luminaries of scholarship from whom we have all
learned. And by the immense range of his studies and his persistent
questioning of the accepted values, he gave us an example of intellectual seriousness, rare among scholars today.[1]*

Meyer Schapiro

Ananda Coomaraswamy was a much more public figure than
René Guénon. Despite his aversion to biography his life story
has been told in some detail by Roger Lipsey. Whitall Perry has
observed of this paradox:

> It nonetheless remains, as Coomaraswamy would doubtless
> have admitted, that biographies of great men are a source
> of inspiration.... While he understandably deplored the
> fashion of modern biography to 'psychoanalyse' the subject
> by dredging up and then distorting trivia, as 'a vulgar cater-
> ing to illegitimate curiosity', this is but the perversion of a
> legitimate art....[2]

The 'legitimate art' has been admirably pursued by Dr Lipsey
in a model biography, sympathetic but clear-eyed and critical,
painstakingly researched but not burdened with trivial detail,
shunning any half-baked psychologizing, narrated in elegant

1. Letter to Doña Luisa Coomaraswamy, September 12, 1947, quoted in R.
Lipsey, *Coomaraswamy: Life and Work* (Princeton: Princeton University, 1977),
p246.
2. W. Perry, 'The Bollingen Coomaraswamy Papers and Biography', *Studies in
Comparative Religion*, 11:4, p212.

prose, and attuned to those aspects of the *oeuvre* to which Coomaraswamy himself would have wished attention to be drawn.

Here we shall concern ourselves less with biographical matter than with an introduction to Coomaraswamy's ideas and writings, focusing on certain intellectual and spiritual contours in Coomaraswamy's development, isolating some landmarks, and offering a few remarks about the influence and significance of his work. It should be said plainly at the outset that nothing less than a full-length study could do justice to the scope and depth of his work nor to the manifold influences issuing from it. By the end of his life Coomaraswamy was thoroughly versed in the scriptures, mythology, doctrines and arts of many different cultures and traditions. He was an astonishingly erudite scholar, a recondite thinker, and a distinguished linguist. He was a prodigious writer, a full bibliography running to upwards of a thousand items on geology, aesthetics and art history, linguistics and philology, social theory, psychology, mythology, folklore, religion, and metaphysics. He lived in three continents and maintained many contacts, both personal and professional, with scholars, antiquarians, artists, theologians, and spiritual practitioners from all over the globe. The contributors to a memorial volume, some hundred and fifty of them, included eminent scholars like A.L. Basham, Joseph Campbell and V.S. Naravane, writers such as T.S. Eliot and Aldous Huxley, art historians like Herman Goetz and Richard Ettinghausen, the distinguished Sanskritist Dr V. Raghavan—the list might go on.[1] Coomaraswamy was a widely known and influential figure. The contrast with Guénon is marked.

We can discern in Coomaraswamy's life and work three focal points which shaped his ideas and writings: a concern with social and political questions connected with the conditions of daily life and work, and with the problematic relationship of the

---

1. See the list of contributors to the memorial volume edited by S.S.D Singam, *Ananda Coomaraswamy, Remembering and Remembering* (Kuala Lumpur: privately published, 1974), pvii.

present to the past and of the 'East' to the 'West'; a fascination with traditional arts and crafts which impelled an immense and ambitious scholarly enterprise; and thirdly, an emerging preoccupation with religious and metaphysical questions which were resolved in a 'unique balance of metaphysical conviction and scholarly erudition.'[1] Allowing some over-simplification, we can distinguish three 'roles' in Coomaraswamy's intellectual life: social commentator and Indologist; historian of Asian art; perennial philosopher. Each of these roles was dominant during a certain period in his life: 1900 to 1917, 1918 to 1932, and 1933 to 1947 respectively. The three strands eventually became interwoven in Coomaraswamy's life and his work. However, his early concerns took on a different character when, following his encounter with the work of Guénon, Coomaraswamy arrived at a thoroughly traditional understanding.

Early Life and the
Ceylon Social Reform Society

Born in Ceylon in 1877 of a Tamil father and an English mother, Coomaraswamy was brought up in England following the early death of his father. He was educated at Wycliffe College and at London University where he studied botany and geology. As part of his doctoral research Coomaraswamy carried out a scientific survey of the mineralogy of Ceylon and seemed poised for a distinguished academic career as a geologist. However, while engaged in field work, his interests took another turn. He became absorbed in a study of the traditional arts and crafts of Ceylon and of the social conditions under which they had been produced. In turn he became increasingly distressed by the corrosive effects of British colonialism.

In 1906 Coomaraswamy founded the Ceylon Social Reform Society of which he was the inaugural President and moving

---

1. Roger Lipsey quoted in W. Perry, 'The Bollingen Coomaraswamy Papers', p206.

force. The Society addressed itself to the preservation and revival not only of traditional arts and crafts but also the social values and customs which had helped to shape them. The Society dedicated itself, in the words of its Manifesto, to discouraging 'the thoughtless imitation of unsuitable European habits and custom.'[1] Coomaraswamy called for a re-awakened pride in Ceylon's past and in her cultural heritage. The fact that he was half-English in no way blinkered his view of the impoverishment of national life brought by the British presence in both Ceylon and India. In both tone and substance the following passage is characteristic of Coomaraswamy in this early period:

> How different it might be if we Ceylonese were bolder and more independent, not afraid to stand on our own legs, and not ashamed of our nationalities. Why do we not meet the wave of European civilisation on equal terms? . . . Our Eastern civilisation was here 2,000 years ago; shall its spirit be broken utterly before the new commercialism of the West? Sometimes I think the eastern spirit is not dead, but sleeping, and may yet play a greater part in the world's spiritual life.[2]

Prescient words indeed in 1905!

In the years between 1900 and 1913 Coomaraswamy moved backwards and forwards between Ceylon, India and England. In India he formed close relationships with the Tagore family and was involved in both the literary renaissance and the *swadeshi* movement.[3] All the while in the subcontinent he was researching the past, investigating arts and crafts, uncovering forgotten and neglected schools of religious and court art, writing scholarly and popular works, lecturing, and organizing bodies such as the Ceylon Social Reform Society and, in England, the India Society.

---

1. Manifesto of the Ceylon Reform Society, almost certainly written by Coomaraswamy, quoted in R. Lipsey, *Coomaraswamy*, p22.

2. A.K. Coomaraswamy *Borrowed Plumes* (1905), quoted in W. Perry, 'The Bollingen Coomaraswamy Papers', p214.

3. See R. Lipsey, *Coomaraswamy*, p75 ff.

In England he found his own social ideas anticipated in the work of William Blake, John Ruskin, and William Morris, three of the foremost representatives of a fiercely eloquent and morally impassioned current of anti-industrialism. Such figures had elaborated a trenchant critique of the ugliest and most dehumanizing aspects of the industrial revolution and of the acquisitive commercialism which increasingly polluted both public and private life. They believed the new values and patterns of urbanization and industrialization were disfiguring the human spirit. These writers, and others like Thomas Carlyle, Charles Dickens, and Matthew Arnold, had protested vehemently against the conditions in which many were forced to carry out their daily work and living. Ruskin and Morris, in particular, were appalled by the debasing of standards of craftsmanship and of public taste. Coomaraswamy picked up a catch-phrase of Ruskin's which he was to mobilize again and again in his own writings: 'industry without art is brutality.' This was more than a glib slogan and signals one of the key themes in Coomaraswamy's work. For many years he was to remain preoccupied with questions about the reciprocal relationships between the conditions of daily life and work, the art of a period, and the social and spiritual values governing the civilisation in question.

The Arts and Crafts Movement of the Edwardian era was, in large measure, stimulated by the ideas of William Morris, the artist, designer, poet, medievalist and social theorist. Morris's work influenced Coomaraswamy decisively in this period and he involved himself with others in England who were trying to put some of Morris's ideas into practice. The Guild and School of Handicraft, with which Coomaraswamy had some connections, was a case in point.[1] (Lipsey does not altogether grasp the moral values which underpinned the Arts and Crafts Movement's resistance to industrialism and speaks of Coomaraswamy's

---

1. Lipsey offers a persuasive discussion of the influence of Morris. For other material on this phase of Coomaraswamy's life and his involvement in the Arts and Crafts movement see pieces by W. Shewring and A. Crawford in *Ananda Coomaraswamy, Remembering and Remembering*.

'absurdly anachronistic' attitude on many social questions in this period.)[1]

We can catch resonances from the work of the anti-industrialists in a passage such as this, written by Coomaraswamy in 1915:

> If the advocates of compulsory education were sincere, and by education meant education, they would be well aware that the first result of any real education would be to rear a race who would refuse point-blank the greater part of the activities offered by present day civilized existence... life under Modern Western culture is not worth living, except for those strong enough and well enough equipped to maintain a perpetual guerilla warfare against all the purposes and idols of that civilisation with a view to its utter transformation.[2]

This articulates a concern with the purposes of education which was to remain with Coomaraswamy all his life. The tone of this passage, ardent and sharp-edged, is typical of Coomaraswamy's writings on social subjects in this period.

Later in life Coomaraswamy turned less often to explicitly social and political questions. By then he had become aware that 'politics and economics, although they cannot be ignored, are the most external and least part of our problem.'[3] However, he never surrendered the conviction that an urbanized and highly industrialized society controlled by materialistic values was profoundly inimical to human development. He was always ready to pull a barbed shaft from his literary quiver when provoked. As late as 1943 we find him writing to *The New English Weekly*, again on the subject of education, in terms no less caustic than those of earlier years:

---

1. R. Lipsey, *Coomaraswamy*, p113. (Lipsey likewise fails to fathom Coomaraswamy's attitude to modern art.)

2. A.K. Coomaraswamy, 'Love and Art', 1915, quoted in R. Lipsey, *Coomaraswamy*, p105.

3. A.K. Coomaraswamy quoted in D. Riepe, *Indian Philosophy and Its Impact on American Thought* (Springfield: Charles C. Thomas, 1970), p126.

We cannot pretend to culture until by the phrase 'standard of living' we come to mean a qualitative standard.... Modern education is designed to fit us to take our place in the counting-house and at the chain-belt; a real culture breeds a race of men able to ask, What kind of work is worth doing?[1]

Coomaraswamy's work on social theory has, as yet, received scant attention.[2] It has been overshadowed by his work as an art historian and as a metaphysician. This is right and proper but it should be remembered that Coomaraswamy was profoundly concerned with social questions throughout his life. These came to be situated in a wider perspective but his concern for a qualitative standard of living runs like a thread through his work.

Coomaraswamy's significance as a social commentator is not fully revealed until his later work when the political and social insights from the early period in his life found their proper place within an all-embracing framework which allowed him to elaborate what Juan Adolpho Vasquez has called 'a metaphysics of culture'.[3] In the years before he moved to America he was more significant as a propagandist and educator than as a theorist. In this respect he was almost certainly more important in India and Ceylon than in England where his voice was one amongst many. The seeds sown by Coomaraswamy in India and Ceylon, at first with his early writings and later through his mature work, have been a long time germinating. The harvest, if it does come, could be none the less rich for that. We should not imagine that because he at first received a lukewarm or even

---

1. Letter to *The New English Weekly*, April 1943, *Selected Letters of Ananda Coomaraswamy*, ed. R.P. Coomaraswamy and A. Moore, Jr, (New Delhi: Oxford, 1988), p293.

2. Two of his most important essays in this field were re-published in *The Bugbear of Literacy*, (London: Perennial Books, 1979) while *Spiritual Authority and Temporal Power in the Indian Theory of Government* was reprinted in 1994 (New York: Oxford).

3. See J.A. Vasquez, 'A Metaphysics of Culture' in *Ananda Coomaraswamy, Remembering and Remembering*.

unfavorable response from his compatriots (an attitude which in some measure persists to this day) that this betokened any kind of failure but rather that his ideas were then, just as his later writings are now, from one point of view, 'ahead of their time.' Ultimately Coomaraswamy's most important function as a social commentator lay in his insistence on relating social and political questions back to underlying religious and metaphysical principles. In this respect he anticipates some of the more percipient of present-day social critics who realize that our most fundamental problems derive from a progressive etiolation of authentic spiritual values. If Guénon's disillusionment with contemporary civilisation was first fashioned by French occultism, Coomaraswamy's was impelled by the contrast between the traditional and the modern industrial cultures of the two countries to which he belonged by birth. His thought was also imprinted with the social concerns and values of the great English anti-industrialists from Blake to Morris.

Pioneering Historian of Asian Art

The second refrain in Coomaraswamy's life is closely related to his interest in social questions and became the dominant theme of his public career: his work as an art historian. From the outset Coomaraswamy's interest in art was fuelled by much more than either antiquarian or 'aesthetic' considerations. For him the most humble folk art and the loftiest religious creations alike were an outward expression not only of the sensibilities of those who created them but of the whole civilisation in which they were nurtured. There was nothing of the *art nouveau* slogan of 'art for art's sake' in Coomaraswamy's outlook. His interest in traditional arts and crafts, from a humble pot to a medieval cathedral, was always governed by the conviction that something immeasurably precious and vitally important was disappearing under the onslaught of modernism in its many different guises. As his biographer remarks, 'history of art was never for him either a light question—one that had only to do with pleasures—or a question of scholarship for its own sake, but

rather a question of setting right what had gone amiss partly
through ignorance of the past.'[1] Coomaraswamy's achievement
as an art historian can perhaps best be understood in respect of
three of the major tasks which he undertook: the 'rehabilitation'
of Asian art in the eyes of Europeans and Asians alike; the massive scholarly labors which he pursued as curator of the Indian
Section of the Boston Museum of Fine Arts; the penetration and
explanation of traditional views of art and their relationship to
philosophy, religion and metaphysics. Again, for purposes of
convenience we can loosely associate each of these tasks with
the three main phases in his adult life whilst remembering that
it was in the middle years (1917–1932) that he devoted himself
almost exclusively to art scholarship.

In assessing Coomaraswamy's achievement it needs to be
remembered that the conventional attitude of the Edwardian
era towards the art of Asia was, at best, condescending, and at
worst, frankly contemptuous. Asian art was often dismissed as
'barbarous', 'second-rate', and 'inferior', and there was a good
deal of foolish talk about 'eight-armed monsters' and the like. In
short, there was, in England at least, an almost total ignorance of
the sacred iconographies of the East. Such an artistic illiteracy
was coupled with a similar incomprehension of traditional philosophy and religion, and buttressed by all manner of Eurocen-
tric assumptions. Worse still was the fact that such attitudes had
infected the Indian intelligentsia, exposed as it was to Western
education and influences.

Following the early days of his fieldwork in Ceylon, Coomaraswamy set about dismantling these prejudices through an affirmation of the beauty, integrity and spiritual density of
traditional art in Ceylon and India and, later, in other parts of
Asia. He was bent on the task of affirming an artistic heritage at
least the equal of Europe's. He not only wrote and spoke and
organized tirelessly to educate the British but he scourged the
Indian intelligentsia for being duped by assumptions of European cultural superiority. In studies like *Medieval Sinhalese Art*

1. R. Lipsey, *Coomaraswamy*, p20.

(1908), *The Arts and Crafts of India and Ceylon* (1913), and his earliest collection of essays, *The Dance of Shiva* (1918), Coomaraswamy combated the prejudices of the age and elaborated an inspiring vision of traditional Indian art and life. He revolutionized several specific fields of art history, radically changed others. His work on Sinhalese arts and crafts and on Rajput painting, though they can now be seen as formative in the light of his later work on Buddhist iconography and on Indian, Platonic and Christian theories of art, were nevertheless early signs of a prodigious scholarship. His influence was not only felt in the somewhat rarefied domain of art history but percolated into other scholarly fields and eventually must have had some influence on popular attitudes in Ceylon, India, England and America.[1]

As a Curator at the Boston Museum Coomaraswamy performed a mighty labour in classifying, cataloguing and explaining thousands of items of oriental art. Through his professional work, his writings, lectures and personal associations Coomaraswamy left an indelible imprint on the work of many American galleries and museums and influenced a wide range of curators, art historians, orientalists and critics—Stella Kramrisch, Walter Andrae, and Heinrich Zimmer to name a few of the more well-known.

Let us now turn to some of the cardinal ideas in Coomaraswamy's understanding of art. Traditional art, he believed, was always directed towards a twin purpose: a daily utility, what he was fond of calling 'the satisfaction of present needs', and the preservation and transmission of moral values and spiritual teachings derived from the tradition in which it appeared. A Tibetan *thanka*, a medieval cathedral, a Red Indian utensil, a Javanese puppet, a Hindu deity image, a piece of Shaker furniture—in such artifacts and creations Coomaraswamy sought a symbolic vocabulary. The intelligibility of traditional arts and crafts, he insisted, does not depend on a more or less precarious

---

1. See articles by Betty Heiman, K.C. Kamaliah, A. Ranganathan, B.N. Goswamy, and M.S. Randhava in *Ananda Coomaraswamy, Remembering and Remembering*.

'recognition', as does modern art, but on 'legibility'. Traditional art does not deal in the private vision of the artist but in a symbolic language.[1]

By contrast, modern Western art (which from a traditional perspective is to say, post-medieval art) is, by contrast, divorced from higher values, tyrannized by the mania for 'originality', controlled by 'aesthetic' (sentimental) considerations, and drawn from the subjective resources of the individual artist rather than from the well-springs of tradition. The comparison, needless to say, does not reflect well on modern art! An example:

> Our artists are 'emancipated' from any obligation to eternal verities, and have abandoned to tradesmen the satisfaction of present needs. Our abstract art is not an iconography of transcendental forms but the realistic picture of a disintegrated mentality.[2]

Art and Metaphysics

During the late 1920s Coomaraswamy's life and work somewhat altered their trajectory. The collapse of his third marriage, ill-health and a growing awareness of death, an impatience with the constrictions of purely academic scholarship, and the influence of René Guénon all deepened Coomaraswamy's interest in spiritual and metaphysical questions.[3] He became more austere in his personal lifestyle, partially withdrew from the academic and social milieu in which he had moved freely over the last decade, and addressed himself to the understanding and explication of traditional metaphysics, especially those of classical

---

1. See A. Coomaraswamy, *Christian and Oriental Philosophy of Art* (New York: Dover, 1956).

2. 'Symptom, Diagnosis and Regimen' in A. Coomaraswamy, *Selected Papers, vol. 1, Traditional Art and Symbolism*, ed. R. Lipsey (Princeton: Princeton University Press, 1977), pp 316–317.

3. See R. Lipsey, *Coomaraswamy*, pp 161–175. On Coomaraswamy's move from 'descriptive iconography' to metaphysics, see his letter to Herman Goetz, June 1939, in *Selected Letters*, pp 26–27.

India and pre-Renaissance Europe. He remarked in one of his letters that 'my indoctrination with the *Philosophia Perennis* is primarily Oriental, secondarily Mediaeval, and thirdly classic.'[1] His later work is densely textured with references to Plato and Plotinus, Augustine and Aquinas, Eckhart and the Rhenish mystics, to Sankara and Lao-Tse and Nagarjuna. He also immersed himself in folklore and mythology since these too carried profound teachings. Coomaraswamy remained the consummate scholar but his work took on a more urgent nature after 1932. He spoke of his 'vocation'—and he was not one to use such words lightly—as 'research in the field of the significance of the universal symbols of the *Philosophia Perennis*' rather than as 'one of apology for or polemic on behalf of doctrines.'[2]

The influence of Guénon was decisive. Coomaraswamy discovered Guénon's writings through Heinrich Zimmer some time in the late twenties and, a few years later, wrote,

> no living writer in modern Europe is more significant than René Guénon, whose task it has been to expound the universal metaphysical tradition that has been the essential foundation of every past culture, and which represents the indispensable basis for any civilisation deserving to be so-called.[3]

Several commentators have detailed the creative reciprocal influences which flowed between Coomaraswamy and Guénon.[4] We shall not go over this ground again here. However, it is worth noting that Coomaraswamy told one of his friends that he and Guénon were 'entirely in agreement on metaphysical

---

1. Letter to Artemus Packard, May 1941, *Selected Letters*, p299.
2. A.K. Coomaraswamy, 'The Bugbear of Democracy, Freedom and Equality', *Studies in Comparative Religion*, 11:3, 1977, p134.
3. Quoted in R. Lipsey, *Coomaraswamy*, p170.
4. See W. Perry, 'Coomaraswamy: The Man and the Witness', in *Ananda Coomaraswamy, Remembering and Remembering*, pp3–7; M. Pallis, 'A Fateful Meeting of Minds: A.K. Coomaraswamy and René Guénon', *Studies in Comparative Religion*, 12:3–4, 1978, pp176–182; and M. Bastriocchi, 'The Last Pillars of Wisdom', in *Ananda Coomaraswamy, Remembering and Remembering*, pp350–359.

principles,' which, of course, did not preclude some divergences of opinion over the applications of these principles on the phenomenal plane.[1]

The vintage Coomaraswamy of the later years is to be found in his masterly works on Vedanta and on the Catholic scholastics and mystics. Some of his work is labyrinthine and not easy of access. It is often laden with a mass of technical detail and with linguistic and philological subtleties which test the patience of some readers. Of his own methodology as an exponent of metaphysics Coomaraswamy wrote,

> We write from a strictly orthodox point of view... endeavouring to speak with mathematical precision, but never employing words of our own, or making any affirmation for which authority could not be cited by chapter and verse; in this way making our technique characteristically Indian.[2]

Sometimes one wishes the chapter and verse documentation was not quite so overwhelming! Coomaraswamy was much more scrupulous than Guénon in this respect, the latter sometimes ignoring the niceties of scholarship at the cost of exposing some of his claims to criticism.

However formidable some of Coomaraswamy's later writings may be they demand close attention from anyone seriously interested in the subjects about which he wrote. There is no finer exegesis of traditional Indian metaphysics than is to be found in Coomaraswamy's later works. His work on the Platonic, Christian and Indian conceptions of sacred art is also unrivalled. Roger Lipsey performed an invaluable service in bringing some of Coomaraswamy's finest essays on these subjects together in *Coomaraswamy, Vol II: Selected Papers, Metaphysics*. Special mention should be made of 'The Vedanta and Western Tradition', 'Sri Ramakrishna and Religious Tolerance', 'Recollection,

---

1. W. Perry, 'Coomaraswamy, 'The Man and the Witness', p5.
2. Quoted in V.S. Naravane, 'Ananda Coomaraswamy: A Critical Appreciation', in *Ananda Coomaraswamy, Remembering and Remembering*, p206.

Indian and Platonic', 'On the One and Only Transmigrant', and 'On The Indian and Traditional Psychology, or Rather Pneumatology'... but it hardly matters what one picks up from the later period: all his mature work is stamped with rare scholarship, elegant expression and a depth of understanding which makes most of the other scholarly work on the same subjects look vapid and superficial. Of his later books three in particular deserve much wider attention: *Christian and Oriental Philosophy of Art* (1939), *Hinduism and Buddhism* (1943), and *Time and Eternity* (1947). *The Bugbear of Literacy* (1979) (first published in 1943 as *Am I my Brother's Keeper?*) and three posthumous collections of some of his most interesting and more accessible essays, *Sources of Wisdom* (1981), *What is Civilisation?* (1989), and *The Essential Coomaraswamy* (2005), offer splendid starting-points for uninitiated readers.

*

Our introductory sketch of Coomaraswamy makes it clear enough that he was a man of wide interests and achievements. From a perennialist point of view we can unhesitatingly ratify Coomaraswamy's own words: 'I have little doubt that my later work, developed out of and necessitated by my earlier works on the arts and dealing with Indian philosophy and Vedic exegesis, is really the most mature and most important part of my work.'[1] However, we should remember that Coomaraswamy's influence radiated out in many directions. Even a severely attenuated list of some of the well-known figures on whom he exercised a significant influence testifies to his impact: Eric Gill, the English designer and writer; Christmas Humphreys, the English judge and early popularizer of Buddhism in England; the great Indologist and Orientalist Heinrich Zimmer; Joseph Campbell, the Jungian student of the world's mythologies; René Guénon himself; Joseph Epes Brown who has helped to bring to light some of the esoteric traditions of the American Indians; the comparative religionist Mircea Eliade; and, of course, other traditionalists

1. In R. Lipsey, *Coomaraswamy*, p248.

such as Titus Burckhardt, Marco Pallis, and Whitall Perry. A tribute from his friend Eric Gill will leave us at an appropriate point to conclude:

> there was one person ... to whose influence I am deeply grateful; I mean the philosopher and theologian, Ananda Coomaraswamy. Others have written the truth about life and religion and man's work. Others have written good clear English. Others have had the gift of witty exposition. Others have understood the metaphysics of Christianity and others have understood the metaphysics of Hinduism and Buddhism. Others have understood the true significance of erotic drawings and sculptures. Others have seen the relationships of the true and the good and the beautiful. Others have had apparently unlimited learning. Others have loved; others have been kind and generous. But I know of no one else in whom all these gifts and all these powers have been combined. ... I believe that no other living writer has written the truth in matters of art and life and religion and piety with such wisdom and understanding.[1]

Whatever we may think of Gill's commendations we can hardly doubt that the life and work of this 'warrior for dharma'[2] was a rare and precious gift to all those interested in the ways of the spirit.

1. E. Gill, *Autobiography* (London: Jonathan Cape, 1940), p174.
2. M. Pallis, 'A Fateful Meeting of Minds', p187.

Rudolf Otto, the East, and Religious Inclusivism

We in the West now realize that we have no monopoly of religious truth. We must in honesty change our attitude towards other faiths, for our watchword must be 'Loyalty to truth'. This changed attitude, however, does not weaken, but rather, instead, reinforces one's faith in God, for He is seen to be not a small or partial being but the Great God who is working throughout all times and places and faiths.[1]

Rudolf Otto

In 1958 the appearance of the second English edition of Rudolf Otto's *The Idea of the Holy* prompted *The London Quarterly Review* to commend the work as 'an acknowledged classic.'[2] In the previous year Mircea Eliade had written of the 'extraordinary interest aroused all over the world' by *Das Heilege*, following its initial publication in 1917.[3] In the inter-war years it was indeed widely read and for a while Otto's theological influence matched that of Karl Barth whose *Römerbrief* (*Commentary on the Letter to the Romans*, 1923) had taken Europe by storm. But since these acclamations Otto's star has somewhat waned. Mark Twain observed that a 'classic' is a book which everyone praises and no one reads. This would now seem to be the fate of Rudolf Otto's best-known work; as Eric Sharpe wittily observed, *The Idea of the Holy* is a book that nearly every comparative religionist imagines

---

1. R. Otto, 'Parallelisms in the Development of Religion East and West', *Transactions of the Asiatic Society of Japan*, 40, 1912, quoted in P. Almond, 'Rudolf Otto and Buddhism', in P. Masefield & D. Wiebe (eds), *Aspects of Religion: Essays in Honor of Ninian Smart*, (New York: Peter Lang, 1994), p69.

2. *LQR* quoted on back cover, R. Otto, *The Idea of the Holy*, tr. J. Harvey (Oxford: Oxford University, 1958). All subsequent references are to this edition.

3. M. Eliade, *The Sacred and the Profane: The Nature of Religion* (New York: 1959), p8.

she/he has read.[1] Less familiar are Otto's later writings on Eastern traditions and his efforts, both theoretical and practical, to fashion a new religious inclusivism and a spirit of harmonious cooperation amongst the world's faiths. After a brief survey of Otto's life and works and some remarks about *The Idea of the Holy*, this article focuses on Otto's encounters with Eastern religious traditions. It also draws attention to his efforts to form the *Religiöser Menschheitbund* (Interreligious League) which aimed to bring together representatives of all the world's religions to work towards international peace, social justice and moral progress, and foregrounds Otto's reconciliation of Christian theology and religious universalism.[2]

Rudolf Otto's Life and Work

Otto was born in 1869 in Northern Germany, into a strict Lutheran family, the twelfth of thirteen children.[3] He describes the family milieu as 'strictly burgherly and small town' and his school education as 'not so pleasant and delightful as it otherwise usually is', due perhaps to his lack of friends and his 'indifference' to the activities of his school mates. At quite a young age he determined to become a pastor and took a keen interest 'in everything ecclesiastical and theological that managed to

---

1. E. Sharpe, *Comparative Religion* (London: Duckworth, 1975), p161.

2. Portions of this article previously appeared in chapter 3 of Harry Oldmeadow, *Journeys East: 20th Century Western Encounters with Eastern Religious Traditions* (Bloomington: World Wisdom, 2004).

3. Otto never wrote about his own life in any detail but did compose an autobiographical sketch in 1891, recently translated and published as 'My Life' in *Autobiographical and Social Essays*, ed. G.D. Alles, (Berlin: Mouton de Gruyter, 1996), pp50–61. In this same work can be found autobiographical excerpts from some of Otto's letters as well as previously untranslated articles on social and political subjects. A short biographical sketch of Otto can be found in H. Turner & P. Mackenzie, *Commentary on 'The Idea of the Holy'* (Aberdeen: Aberdeen Peoples Press, no date). A fuller biographical account can be found in E. Benz (ed), *Rudolf Otto's Bedeutung für die Religionswissenschaft und die Theologie Heute* (Leiden: E.J. Brill, 1971).

appear within my narrow horizons.'[1] Otto studied theology, languages, music and art at the universities of Erlangen and Göttingen. The young theologian was disenchanted with the 'ossified intellectualism' of the prevailing rationalistic theology and was strongly attracted to Martin Luther's insistence that the knowledge of God has little to do with the rational faculties.[2] Indeed, Otto's dissertation for his licentiate in theology was on Luther's view of the Holy Spirit and he repeatedly returned to the Pauline maxim that 'the letter killeth but the spirit giveth life.' Otto was also much influenced in his early years by Kant, Schleiermacher, Fries, Albrecht Ritschl, and Ernest Troeltsch, each of whom provided a strong antidote to the regnant theological orthodoxies of the period. In 1899 Otto edited a centennial edition of Schleiermacher's *Speeches on Religion* and a decade later published his first major work, *The Philosophy of Religion based on Kant and Fries*. Otto was swimming against the tide of enthusiasm for the theology of Rudolf Bultmann, Karl Barth and Emil Brunner, one which 'overwhelmed Otto at the pinnacle of his career, and resulted in a widespread rejection of his work among theologians.'[3] Nearly half a century later Karl Barth recalled this uncongenial climate:

> Everything that even from afar smelt of mysticism and morals, of pietism and romanticism or even idealism, how suspect it was and how strictly prohibited or confined in the straitjacket of restrictions.[4]

In similar vein Paul Tillich later recalled his years at Marburg in 1924–25:

> During the three semesters of my teaching I met the first radical effects of the neo-orthodox theology on theology

---

1. R. Otto, 'My Life', pp 51–52.
2. J. Wach, *Types of Religious Experience, Christian and Non-Christian* (Chicago: University of Chicago Press, 1951), p213.
3. G. Alles, in *Autobiographical and Social Essays*, p 9.
4. Barth quoted in *Autobiographical and Social Essays*, p 9.

students: cultural problems were excluded from theological thought; theologians like Schleiermacher, Harnack, Troeltsch, Otto, were contemptuously rejected; social and political ideas were banned from theological discussions.[1]

Otto trained for the Lutheran ministry and after two years in a theological seminary he traveled to the Middle East. In Cairo he was profoundly influenced by the Coptic liturgy, by some Jewish rites in Jerusalem and by a Dervish ceremony which he described as 'unspeakable'. After these experiences, formative in his intellectual and spiritual development, he returned to Germany via the great monastic center at Mt Athos where he spent ten days. This trip provided the catalyst for his great intellectual enterprise—the construction of 'a methodology of religious feeling.'

Otto's professional life, apart from brief stints in the Lutheran ministry and as a member of the Prussian Parliament, was as an academic systematic theologian. He was appointed to a position at Göttingen University in 1898 where he worked before moving as a full professor to Breslau in 1915, and three years later to Marburg where he succeeded the illustrious Wilhelm Herrmann. He wrote on a wide range of religious subjects and lectured at many universities on both sides of the Atlantic. Joachim Wach has left us a vivid pen portrait of Otto in his later years:

> Rudolf Otto was an imposing figure. He held himself straight and upright. His movements were measured. The sharply cut countenance kept a grave expression which did not change much even when jesting. The color of his skin was yellowish-white and betrayed past illness. Otto had contracted a tropical disease in India which forced him ever after to husband his strength strictly. His hair was white and clipped.... A small white moustache covered his upper lip. His most fascinating features were his steel-blue eyes. There was a rigidity in his glance, and one had the impression that he was 'seeing' something, as he spoke, to which his inter-

1. Tillich quoted in *Autobiographical and Social Essays*, 4n.

locutor had no access.... An air of genuine mystery sur-
rounded Otto. Familiarity was the last thing which a visitor
would have expected of the great scholar or he himself
would have encouraged. The students who followed his lectures tensely and with awe called him the Saint...neither
before nor since my meeting Otto have I known a person
who impressed one more genuinely as a true mystic. There
was something about him of the solitude into which an intimate communion with the Divine has frequently led those
who were favoured in this way.[1]

Throughout his adult life Otto was engaged in a range of
extra-academic activities—the movement for liturgical and
ecclesiastical reform (including the creation of ministries for
women), electoral change and efforts to establish an international Religious League. Ill health forced Otto's early retirement
in 1929. He died of pneumonia in 1937, shortly after suffering an
almost fatal sixty-foot fall from a tower which he had climbed in
Staufenberg. The last years of his life were marred by severe illness, morphine addiction, depression, and perhaps more severe
psychiatric disturbance; it is possible that Otto's 'fall' was a sui-
cide attempt.[2] The inscription on Otto's tomb in Marburg is
'Heilig, Heilig, Heilig, ist der Herr Zaboath', the sanctus which had
taken on a particular resonance in his life and work.
    Nine of Otto's books appeared in English in the interwar
years but many of his essays have only recently appeared in
English, thanks to the enterprise of Gregory Alles. Otto's work
falls quite neatly into two distinct periods: the early years of his
professional life in which he was engrossed in teaching and
writing about Protestant theology; and the later years in which
his attention often turned Eastwards and towards more universal religious problems and themes. The Idea of the Holy is a kind of
fulcrum between these two periods. Throughout his adult life
he also wrote many articles on social and political subjects.

1. J. Wach, Types of Religious Experience, pp210–211.
2. See P. Almond, Rudolf Otto: An Introduction to His Philosophical Theology
(Chapel Hill: University of North Carolina, 1984), pp24–25.

The Idea of the Holy

Das heilege appeared in 1917, in Europe a year of war, revolution, widespread dislocation, a mood of confusion, anxiety and nihilism. It was to become one of the century's most influential books on the nature of religious experience, in some ways a descendant of William James' *The Varieties of Religious Experience* (1902). Soon translated into all the major European languages it was immensely popular in the decade after its publication, perhaps because it answered to something in the mood of the times.[1]

The Idea of the Holy was an attempt to establish a category under which religious experience could be understood in its own right, free of any theoretical schema imported from outside. It was also an attempt to valorize the non-rational (as distinct from irrational) elements of religion. Otto's work was attuned to the spirit of Pascal's maxim,

> if one subjects everything to reason our religion will lose its mystery and its supernatural character. If one offends the principles of reason our religion will be absurd and ridiculous.... These are two equally dangerous extremes, to shut reason out and to let nothing else in.[2]

In 1913 Otto's friend, the Swedish theologian Nathan Söderblom, had written, 'Holiness is the great word in religion; it is even more essential than the notion of God.'[3] Otto's purpose was to recuperate the full meaning of the word 'holy' and to take hold of the religious experience to which this word points. Otto believed the word had been contaminated by moral associations which were quite secondary to its fundamental meaning, and

---

1. For a very brief account of *The Idea of the Holy* and its place in the trajectory of Otto's work, see T.M. Ludwig, 'Rudolf Otto', in M. Eliade (ed.), *The Encyclopedia of Religion*, vol. 11 (New York: Simon & Schuster, 1995), pp139–141.

2. See J. Harvey, Translator's Preface, *The Idea of the Holy*, pxix.

3. N. Söderblom, 'Holiness', in J. Hastings (ed), *Encyclopedia of Religion and Ethics*, vol. 6, (Edinburgh: T&T Clark, 1913), p731.

therefore turned instead to an old Latin word, *numen*, to signal the realm of the most profound religious experience. The holy, he wrote, 'is a category peculiar to religion ... [it] is perfectly *sui generis* and irreducible to any other; and therefore, like every absolutely primary and elementary datum, while it admits of being discussed, it cannot be defined,'[1] but only evoked on the basis of experience. To experience the numinous is to encounter the *mysterium tremendum* which is marked by an overpowering sense of otherness, of awfulness, majesty and energy but which is also *fascinans*—beautiful, alluring, captivating. This *real presence*, neither a phantom nor a projection of the sub-conscious but, in Christian terms, the 'living God', calls up 'creaturely feeling' and appears 'in a form ennobled beyond measure where the soul held speechless, trembles inwardly to the furthest fibre of its being.'[2] In an Appendix Otto reproduces the thrilling passage from the *Bhagavad Gita* where Arjuna 'smitten with amazement' beholds the manifold forms of Krishna, more dazzling than 'the light of a thousand suns.'[3]

Part of the book's appeal, for both general reader and for the student of religion, was Otto's understanding of religion primarily in experiential rather than creedal terms. At a time when 'religion' was often thought to hinge on *belief* and *morality* Otto turned attention to the religious *experience*, not to offer any reductionistic 'scientific' explanation but to affirm its mystery and power, and its centrality in religion. Comparative religionists were later to take up Otto's interest in the holy (now more often than not termed 'the sacred') as one of the structuring principles of their inquiries. Unhappily, the very popularity of this germinative work has somewhat obscured Otto's many other achievements, not least in the field of Indological studies and in the promotion of global interreligious understanding.

1. R. Otto, *The Idea of the Holy*, p7.
2. R. Otto, Ibid., p17.
3. R. Otto, Ibid., Appendix 2.

Otto and the East

In 1911 Otto traveled extensively in North Africa, the Middle East, and India: his experiences were to be decisive in the gestation of *The Idea of the Holy*. In a now-famous passage in letter to a German church weekly he described the effect of hearing the *Trisagion* of Isaiah in the synagogue in Moroccan Mogador (now Essaouira):

> It is Sabbath, and already in the dark and inconceivably grimy passage of the house we hear that sing-song of prayers and reading of scripture, that nasal half-singing half-speaking which Church and Mosque have taken over from the Synagogue. The sound is pleasant, one can soon distinguish modulations and cadences that follow one another at regular intervals, like *Leitmotiv*. The ear tries to grasp individual words but it is scarcely possible ... when suddenly out of the babel of voices, causing a thrill of fear, there it begins, unified, clear and unmistakable: *Kadosh Kadosh Kadosh Elohim Adonai Zebaoth Male'u hashamayim wahaarets kebodo!* (Holy, holy, holy, Lord of hosts, the heavens and the earth are full of thy glory.) I have heard the *Sanctus Sanctus Sanctus* of the cardinals in St Peters, the *Swiat Swiat Swiat* in the Cathedral of the Kremlin and the Holy Holy Holy of the Patriarch in Jerusalem. In whatever language they resound, these most exalted words that have ever come from human lips always grip one in the depths of the soul, with a mighty shudder exciting and calling into play the mystery of the other world latent therein. And this more than anywhere else here in this modest place, where they resound in the same tongue in which Isaiah first received them and from the lips of the people whose first inheritance they were.[1]

Of this incident Ernst Benz has written, 'It is particularly noteworthy that Otto came to know the experience [of the holy] not primarily from reading sacred texts but on a journey as a

---

1. From H. Turner & P. Mackenzie, *Commentary on 'The Idea of the Holy'*, p 4. For another translation see R. Otto, *Autobiographical and Social Essays*, pp 80–81.

spontaneous religious experience in a Jewish synagogue in Morocco....'[1] The Asian leg of his journey also left an abiding impression on Otto. Soon after arriving in Karachi he was astonished when a newly-met young Hindu launched into an eloquent discourse on the philosophy of Kant. Otto sailed up the Indus river to Lahore and thence traveled to Calcutta and Orissa where he was lavishly entertained by a Maharajah in whom he found an attractive blend of European learning and Hindu piety. In India he had friendly encounters with Muslims, Sikhs, Hindus and Parsees. From India Otto traveled to Burma where he was much impressed by the vitality of Theravadan Buddhism. In Japan he visited universities, temples, and monasteries and may have been the first Westerner to address a large gathering of Zen monks. He went on to China where he stayed for two months before returning to Europe through Siberia, all the while accumulating priceless religious artifacts for the *Religionskundliche Sammlung* (Museum of the World's Religions) which he had established in Marburg.

Despite poor health Otto returned to India in 1927, partly in order to gather materials for the museum in Marburg, partly to promote the *Religiöser Menschheitsbund* (see below). Otto visited many religious sites throughout the sub-continent; his letters evince a keen and sympathetic interest in the beliefs and practices of the Buddhists, Muslims and Parsees as well as the Hindus. A visit to Elephanta Island (near Bombay), like his earlier experiences in the Middle East, left the most profound impression on him. His oft-cited description:

> One climbs halfway up the mountainside on magnificent stone steps until a wide gate opens on the right, in the volcanic rocks. This leads into one of the mightiest of early Indian rock temples. Heavy pillars hewn out of the rock support the roof. The eye slowly accustoms itself to the semi-darkness, gradually distinguishes awesome representations— carved into the wall—of the religious epics of India, until it

---

1. Benz quoted in *Autobiographical and Social Essays*, p 61.

reaches the imposing central recess. Here an image rises up out of the rock which I can only compare with the great representations of Christ in early Byzantine churches. It is a three-headed form, carved only as far as the breast, in threefold human size.... Still and powerful the central head looks down, with both the others in profile. Over the image rests a perfect peace and majesty.... Nowhere else have I found the secret of the transcendent world, the other world more grandly and perfectly expressed than in these three heads... To see this place were alone worth a journey to India, while from the spirit of religion which has lived here, one may experience more in a single hour of contemplation than from all the books.[1]

The last sentence is a telling sign of Otto's deepening conviction that 'the spirit of religion' transcends all formal boundaries and lies in contemplative experience, beyond the reach of 'all the books.'

Otto was by now an accomplished Sanskritist, had translated several early Vedic texts and had published his most important contribution to Western understanding of the Hindu tradition, *Mysticism East and West* (1926), in which he continued Schopenhauer's association of Vedantic metaphysics and Meister Eckhart's apophatic theology. Whilst not unaware of 'manifold singularities', Otto found in the mystics of both East and West 'an astonishing conformity in the deepest impulses of human

---

1. Quoted in P. Almond, *Rudolf Otto*, pp 23–24. Alternative translation in R. Otto, *Autobiographical and Social Essays*, pp 94–95. For a similar epiphany experienced by a Western Christian in the face of traditional sculptures see Thomas Merton's account of his encounter with the Buddha figures of Polanuwurra (Sri Lanka) in N. Burton et. al. (eds), *The Asian Journal of Thomas Merton* (New York: New Directions, 1972), pp 33–36. Fr Henri Le Saux (Swami Abhishiktananda) was 'thunderstruck' by his encounter with the great figure of Siva Maheswara at Elephanta, describing it as 'one of those high points that light up one's life'; see J. Stewart, *Swami Abhishiktananda: His life through his letters* (Delhi: ISPCK, 2000) p 81, and Abhishiktananda, *Ascent to the Depth of the Heart* (Delhi: ISPCK, 1998), pp 105–106. Fr Bede Griffiths' account of a very similar experience at Elephanta can be found in *The Marriage of East and West* (London: Collins, 1982), pp 10–11.

spiritual experience,' independent of 'race, clime, and age.'[1] As Richard King has noted, Otto's enterprise is colored by his apparent intention to rehabilitate Eckhart's standing within German Protestantism through the comparison with Sankara—an example of 'the projection of Christian theological debates . . . onto an Indian canvas.'[2] Nonetheless, Otto's work remains a pioneering work of remarkable acuity in the field of comparative mysticism.

In *The Idea of the Holy* Otto had already discussed the mystical dimension of religion in terms altogether consonant with the spiritual vocabularies of the East. Take this, for example:

> And as soon as speculative thought has come to concern itself with this . . . type of consciousness. . . . We come upon the ideas, first, of the annihilation of the self, and then, as its complement, of the transcendent as the sole and entire reality. For one of the chiefest and most general features of mysticism is just this *self-depreciation* . . . the estimation of the self, the personal 'I', as something not perfectly or essentially real, or even as a mere nullity, a self-depreciation which comes to demand its own fulfilment in practice in rejecting the delusion of selfhood, and so makes for the annihilation of the self.[3]

After this second trip to India Otto wrote a good many scholarly works on the Vaisnavite tradition, translated several texts, including those of Ramanuja, the *Katha Upanishad* and the *Bhagavad Gita* with which he originally felt little sympathy but on which he was to write with considerable discernment.[4] Otto also wrote another comparison of his own tradition and Hinduism, *India's Religion of Grace and Christianity* (1928). Much of Otto's work

1. R. Otto, *Mysticism East and West: A Comparative Analysis of the Nature of Mysticism* (New York: Meridian Books, 1957), pv.

2. R. King, *Orientalism and Religion: Postcolonial theory, India and 'the mystic East'* (London: Routledge, 1999), p126.

3. *The Idea of the Holy*, p21.

4. See H. Rollmann, 'Rudolf Otto and India', *Religious Studies Review*, 5:3, July 1979, pp199–203. Rollman provides a full bibliography of Otto's Indological writings, some 70-odd in all.

served as a corrective to the Western preoccupation with Advaita Vedanta, often assimilated with the Hindu tradition as a whole. Of Otto's imposing Indological work, Joachim Wach had this to say:

> All these studies not only bespeak an intimate acquaintance with the texts and the philological problems involved in their interpretation, not only a comprehensive knowledge of the theological and philosophical systems of India and of the outstanding Hindu thinkers and teachers, but also a deep understanding of Indian devotion.[1]

Given Otto's deep-seated interest in lived religious experience and his perception of the similarities between the theistic piety of the Abrahamic traditions and Hindu *bhakti,* it comes as no surprise that Wach should identify his understanding of devotion as one of the hallmarks of Otto's Indological works.

Amongst Otto's most interesting and penetrating essays was one on Gandhi, whom Otto recognized as a distinctly Indian type.

> True, Gandhi impresses us through his profound humanity, and we admire 'the human' in him. But he is an Indian, and it is as a great Indian that he is a great person.... We misunderstand Gandhi when we attempt to understand the strong powers and virtues of this man simply in terms of a generalized humanity ... 'the great nationalist', 'the friend of the people', 'a clever politician', 'a born leader'. He is all these things, but he is so as an Indian *sadhu* [renunciate]. He is these things as a result of his situation, but if the situation were different, his character as a *sadhu* would remain the same and would find other ways to express itself.[2]

He also discerned in Gandhi the beneficent influence of the various religions to which he had been exposed and to whose ethical teachings he was peculiarly receptive—Jainism, Islam and Christianity, as well as his own Vaisnavite tradition.[3]

1. J. Wach, *Types of Religious Experience,* p 216.
2. R. Otto, *Autobiographical and Social Essays,* pp 195–196.
3. Ibid., p 203.

Although Otto was most strongly attracted to Hinduism, especially its medieval expressions, he also wrote sympathetically about Buddhism of both the Theravadan and Mahayana traditions. His percipient essay (1924) on Zen Buddhism came at a time when it was virtually unknown in the West and followed his many suggestive references to Buddhism in *The Idea of the Holy*.[1] Philip Almond tells us that Otto was the first German scholar of religion to visit Zen monasteries in Japan where he conversed with Zen masters, practised *zazen*, addressed Zen monks on the affinities of Christianity and Buddhism, and lectured at the Asiatic Society of Japan on parallels between the religions of East and West.[2] At a time when any amount of nonsense was being written in the West about Buddhism Otto's insights were penetrating indeed, and are still illuminating today. A simple example from *The Idea of the Holy*:

> I recall vividly a conversation I had with a Buddhist monk. He had been putting before me methodically and pertinaciously the arguments for the Buddhist 'theology of negation', the doctrine of *Anatman* and 'entire emptiness'. When he had made an end, I asked him, what then *Nirvana* itself is; and after a long pause came at last the single answer, low and restrained: 'Bliss—unspeakable.' And the hushed restraint of that answer, the solemnity of his voice, demeanor, and gesture, made more clear what was meant than the words themselves.[3]

Unlike many of his predecessors and contemporaries Otto did not find Buddhism either 'nihilistic' or 'pessimistic' and in Zen discerned a radical mystical method, 'almost torn away from all rational schemata', aimed at a direct encounter with the

---

1. Arthur Waley's essay 'Zen Buddhism and Its Relation to Art' appeared in 1923 and has been acclaimed as one of the first substantial European writings on Zen. Otto had already written on Zen, not at any great length but with sharp insight, in *Das Heilege*.

2. See P. Almond, 'Rudolf Otto and Buddhism', p60.

3. *The Idea of the Holy*, p39.

numinous, the 'wholly other'.[1] In 1925 Otto wrote the preface to the first book on Zen in German, a collection of classical texts translated by Ohasama Shuei, entitled *Zen: Living Buddhism in Japan*. His later essay, 'Numinous Experience in Zen', has also been heralded as an important work.[2]

Otto's wrote very little on Islam but even here one sees a remarkably plastic religious sensibility at work, one which gave play to spontaneous aesthetic illuminations — a kind of sensibility not always to be found amongst academic theologians! How much of the spiritual economy of Islam Otto is able to evoke in a few deft strokes in his modest notes on 'The empty in Islamic architecture' (1932):

> Mosques are 'empty'. This is often confused with austerity and attributed to the alleged rationalism of Islam and its cultus. To be sure, there are mosques that are very austere, but there are others in which the empty speaks so impressively that it puts a lump in one's throat and takes one's breath away. . . . This high art works with space and through spaces that it orders, divides, and combines. At the same time it works with light, or rather, with half-light, which it wonderfully guides, gradates, mixes, augments, and interrupts. The use of both space and light makes the empty and the quiet meaningful and expressive. It does so without a word and more powerfully than cathedrals filled with images, figures and ritual implements that diffuse, refract, and establish meaning through the all-too-significant and the all-too-conceptual.[3]

In the same essay he describes Islamic calligraphy as 'music with lines' which 'draws the words of the *Qur'an* back into the mystery from which they flowed.'

1. R. Otto, '*Aufsätze das Numinose betreffend*' (1923), quoted in P. Almond, 'Rudolf Otto and Buddhism', p60. See also R. Otto, 'Professor Rudolf Otto on Zen', *The Eastern Buddhist*, 3:2, July–Sept 1924, pp117–125.

2. See H. Dumoulin, *Zen Buddhism in the 20th Century* (New York: Weatherhill, 1992), p5. (This essay is apparently not yet in English translation.)

3. 'Buddhism, Islam and the irrational' (1932), in *Autobiographical and Social Essays*, pp190–191.

Otto often derived his most acute insights from direct existential encounters rather than from his researches in the library. Would that we could say the same of many of today's scholars of religion for whom the phenomena under investigation are just so many laboratory specimens! (As the Romanian philosopher E.M. Cioran remarked, 'One does not imagine a specialist in the history of religions *at prayer*. Or if indeed he does pray...then he ruins his *Treatises*, in which no *true* god figures....')[1] Otto's intellect was as sharp as you like, his scholarship immense and his capacity for argumentation formidable indeed; but perhaps more important than all this, especially in his engagement with Eastern forms, was a kind of intuitive receptivity shared by some of the century's most arresting Western commentators on Eastern religious traditions — one may here mention such names as Mircea Eliade, Thomas Merton and Henri Le Saux (Swami Abhishiktananda).

The Interreligious League

As early as 1913 Otto had conceived the idea of a *Religiöser Menschheitbund* (Interreligious League) which would bring together representatives of all the world's religions to work towards international peace, social justice and moral progress. In the sorry aftermath of World War I Otto pleaded eloquently and passionately for the RMB:

> I hope that the misery which all nations suffer today will finally teach them what religion and ethics should have taught them a long time ago: that they do not walk alone. People of every land and nation must constantly bear in mind that they face great collective tasks, and that to accomplish these tasks they need brotherly collaboration and cooperation. By themselves, political associations cannot do what is needed.... Will [the League of Nations]

---

1. E.M. Cioran, *Anathemas and Admirations* (1947), tr. Richard Howard, (New York: Arcade, 1991), p188.

become anything more than a 'limited liability corporation' that actively pursues the special interests of whatever groups temporarily find themselves in power.... In and of themselves, institutions, laws, decrees, and negotiations are powerless. They require the continual support of an awakened collective conscience....

After commending the efforts of his friend, Swedish Archbishop Nathan Söderblom, to initiate a more lively and fertile Christian ecumenicism (eventually leading to the formation of the World Council of Churches in 1948), Otto went on:

But Christianity hardly encompasses all of humanity.... What would it mean if perhaps every three years those who represent the consciences of individual nations—the most influential leaders and emissaries of all churches all over the world—assembled publicly to discuss issues of universal concern, to display personally their common feeling for all of humanity, and then to take home a heightened will to create a global community? In time this assembly would develop into a forum that would be completely independent of the struggles and limitations of diplomacy. It could discuss the great issues of the day.

Otto's identification of those problems strikes a very contemporary note:

[I]ssues of public and international morality, social and cultural issues that all nations share, unavoidable clashes between different nations and how to alleviate them, issues of class, gender, and race.... The same body would also provide a natural court of appeals for oppressed minorities, classes, and nations.[1]

Under Otto's leadership the RMB, established in 1920, actually flourished for a time and attracted participants from Asia and North America as well as many European countries. Otto's trip

1. R. Otto, *Autobiographical and Social Essays*, p145.

to the subcontinent in 1928–29 was principally to gain support for the RMB, efforts which met with considerable success. It was dissolved in 1933 but was revived by Friedrich Heiler and Karl Küssner in 1956 and thereafter became the German branch of the World Congress of Faiths which had been founded early in the century by Sir Francis Younghusband.[1] Whilst the RMB and its successors have not hitherto realized Otto's lofty ideals, who is foolish enough to say that his vision has no relevance today? In a world riven with all manner of strife, much of it inter-religious, and at the end of the most blood-stained century in recorded history, perhaps it is timely to listen once again to Otto's impassioned words, uttered in the aftermath of the Great War:

> If one could win the 'churches' of the great world religions and their leaders for the cause of the great, common tasks of humanity—ordering relations between nations, classes, races, and genders in accordance with basic human rights; peaceful collaboration instead of war and aggression; reason and orderliness instead of the interests of those who are temporarily in power; the deliberate shaping of destiny instead of blindly allowing nature and destiny to take their course—then there would be created, in universal conviction and united opinion, the spiritual soil from which would grow lasting forms of international law and powerful organizations of nations and classes.[2]

Many will no doubt dismiss Otto's vision as 'sentimental', 'utopian', and the like—that is the fate of visionaries! But an implacable fact remains: Otto's appeal for the development of 'a global conscience', rooted in the recognition of 'the binding force of right and justice as the supreme norms governing relations between individuals and communities', and addressing

---

1. On the life and work of Younghusband see Patrick French, *Younghusband: The Last Great Imperial Adventurer*, (London: HarperCollins, 1994).
2. 'A League of Nations is not enough', *Autobiographical and Social Essays*, p146.

'the great, collective moral tasks'[1] of the age, cannot be indefinitely ignored without imperilling the very future of the human family and, indeed, of our planetary home.

Religious Inclusivism

Over the last century we can discern in the study of religion four distinct approaches, sometimes overlapping: the *rationalistic* perspective which treats religion as any other cultural phenomenon and strives for some sort of quasi-scientific 'objectivity' (actually chimerical—but that is a debate for another occasion); the *theological* outlook which views 'religion' and 'religions' through the lens of a particular religious viewpoint; the *universalist* approach which rests on the notion that behind myriad religious forms lies some sort of common core or essence; and the *phenomenological* method which sets aside all questions relating to 'truth claims' and seeks to allow the 'phenomena' to somehow speak for themselves. Needless to say there are all manner of variations and off-shoots within these broad general groupings. Rudolf Otto is one of the first of a small group of Christian theologians who have attempted to reconcile their own fervently-held religious commitments with a more inclusive and universalist approach in the study of religion. As Seyyed Hossein Nasr observed many years ago, as far as religiously committed scholars are concerned,

> The essential problem that the study of religion poses is how to preserve religious truth, traditional orthodoxy, the dogmatic theological structures of one's own tradition, and yet gain knowledge of other traditions and accept them as spiritually valid ways and roads to God.[2]

Otto squarely faced the fact that Christian exclusivism must give way to a much more open approach to other religions. As

1. Ibid., p149.
2. S.H. Nasr, *Sufi Essays* (London: Allen & Unwin, 1972), p127.

early as 1912 he had struck a prophetic note with these noble words:

> We in the West now realize that we have no monopoly of religious truth. We must in honesty change our attitude towards other faiths, for our watchword must be 'Loyalty to truth'. This changed attitude, however, does not weaken, but rather, instead, reinforces one's faith in God, for He is seen to be not a small or partial being but the Great God who is working throughout all times and places and faiths.[1]

Here Otto anticipates the work of such later figures as W. Cantwell Smith, Klaus Klostermaier, Henri Le Saux, Bede Griffiths, William Johnston, and Diana Eck, in each of whom we find a steadfast commitment to the Christian tradition hand-in-hand with the deepest respect for, interest in and openness to the spiritual modalities of other traditions. But none of this should be confused with the kind of 'universalism' which anticipates the creation of a new 'super-religion'. Otto himself had no interest whatsoever in any kind of syncretism or admixture of religious elements in some sort of ersatz 'universal' religion:

> We most emphatically reject any form of cosmopolitanism in the area of religion.... We maintain our religion and cherish its claims, at the same time that we allow others to advocate their own religion.... We consider the propagation and spreading of our own religion to be one of our most sacred duties....[2]

*

Although Otto's work has been strangely neglected in the Anglophone world over the last fifty years there is no doubting his influence on both theologians and comparative religionists. For many years Paul Tillich alone amongst German theologians really carried Otto's banner in the English-speaking world but

1. R. Otto, 'Parallelisms', p69.
2. 'A League of Nations is not enough', p148.

the climate today, in which 'theologians now inhabit a world of religious pluralism, uncertain truth claims, and interreligious dialogue' may well make Otto's ideas congenial once again.[1] Amongst comparative religionists his legacy was perhaps most evident in the work of his compatriot Joachim Wach but Otto also palpably influenced figures such as Mircea Eliade, Friedrich Heiler, Gerardus van der Leeuw, and Ugo Bianchi. In more recent years scholars such as Philip Almond and Gregory Alles have helped to revive interest in one of the twentieth century's most interesting, imposing and attractive scholars of religion. There can be no doubting that the ideals for which Otto strived and the values he upheld, both within the Church and in the wider world, have lost none of their pertinence or urgency.

1. G. Alles, in R. Otto, *Autobiographical and Social Essays*, p 11.

C.G. Jung &
Mircea Eliade
'Priests without Surplices'?

The decisive question for man is: Is he related to something infinite or not? That is the telling question of his life.[1]   Carl Jung

[T]he history of religions reaches down and makes contact with that which is essentially human: the relation of man to the sacred. The history of religions can play an extremely important role in the crisis we are living through. The crises of modern man are to a large extent religious ones, insofar as they are an awakening of his awareness to an absence of meaning.[2]   Mircea Eliade

[T]he scientific pursuit of religion puts the saddle on the wrong horse, since it is the domain of religion to evaluate science, and not vice versa.[3]   Whitall Perry

Mircea Eliade

The academic study of religion over the last half-century has been hugely influenced by the work of Mircea Eliade. His scholarly *oeuvre* is imposing indeed, ranging from highly specialized monographs to his encyclopedic and magisterial *A History of Religious Ideas*, written in three volumes over the last decade of

1. C.G. Jung, *Memories, Dreams, Reflections* (London: Fontana, 1983), pp356–7.
2. M. Eliade, *Ordeal by Labyrinth, Conversations with Claude-Henri Rocquet* (Chicago: University of Chicago, 1982), p148.
3. W. Perry, Review of N. Smart's *The Phenomenon of Religion* in *Studies in Comparative Religion*, 7:2, 1973, p127.

his life. He was recognized throughout the world, elected to many different Academies, showered with honours. Eliade's erudition was imposing: his own library ran to something over 100,000 volumes and he was certainly not one to buy books for decorative purposes. (I'm told that it is possible in America to buy books by the yard and by color!) Looking back we get a sense, as we do with Carl Jung, of indefatigable labours and colossal output. Both Jung and Eliade were pioneers who changed, respectively, the theoretical landscapes of psychology and comparative religion.

Eliade's attitude to autobiography was much less ambivalent than Jung's and we have to hand four volumes of personal journals and a two-volumed autobiography. With the journals particularly, one sometimes shares the sentiments of the schoolboy who opened his review of a book on elephants with the words, 'This book told me more than I wanted to know about elephants.' Eliade was born in Romania in 1907 and died in Chicago in 1986. His Romanian nationality was a decisive factor in his life and work; from an early age he felt he had one foot in the Occident, the other in the Orient, reflected in the title of the first volume of his autobiography *Journey East, Journey West*. He developed an early interest in folklore, mythology and religion, and learnt English in order to read Max Müller and J.G. Frazer. At university he mastered Hebrew, Persian, and Italian, and embarked on a postgraduate study of the influence of Hermeticism and the Kabbalah on Italian Renaissance philosophy. Whilst visiting Italy he read Dasgupta's famous work *The History of Indian Philosophy*. So deeply affected was he by this work that he soon left for Calcutta to study Indian philosophy and spirituality under Dasgupta. In Calcutta he immersed himself in Sanskrit and classical Indian philosophy, and developed an interest in the psycho-spiritual disciplines of yoga and tantra. He spent six months in the holy city of Rishikesh, at the foot of the Himalayas, under the guidance of Swami Shivananda. After more than three years in the sub-continent he returned to Romania where he took up teaching and writing. His involvement in Romanian fascism has recently come to light and has somewhat tarnished his reputation.[1] Apart from a shadowy interlude during the war when he carried out diplomatic work in Lisbon, Eliade devoted the rest of his life to writing and teaching about religious phenomena. After the Soviet seizure of Romania he settled in Paris and over the next decade moved from one temporary post to another, living a rather hand-to-mouth existence. The Communist takeover of Romania left him in an exile that was to be permanent. His work was denounced in Romania itself as being 'obscurantist', 'mystic', and 'fascist.'[2] (Decoded these words might signify an interest in the past and in religion, and a hostility to Communist totalitarianism.) In the late 40s and early 50s he produced several works which quickly established his international reputation: *Patterns in Comparative Religion, The Myth of the Eternal Return, Shamanism: Archaic Techniques of Ecstasy* and *Yoga: Immortality and Freedom*. In 1956 Eliade was invited to the University of Chicago as a visiting professor. He was to remain there for the rest of his life. When he took up a chair in the History of Religions at Chicago it was one of very few such chairs; within 15 years there were at least 25 chairs in the major American universities, nearly all of them occupied by his former students.[3] Like Jung, Eliade seems to have understood his own role in somewhat prophetic terms. From his *Journal*: 'I feel as though I am a precursor; I am aware of being somewhere in the *avant-garde* of the humanity of tomorrow or after.'[4]

1. Eliade's involvement with the fascist and anti-Semitic Iron Guard has been exposed in Adriana Berger's 'Mircea Eliade: Romanian Fascism and the History of Religions', in *Tainted Greatness: Antisemitism and Cultural Heroes*, ed. Nancy Harrowitz (Philadelphia: Temple University, 1994). See also my *Journeys East* (Bloomington: World Wisdom, 2004), pp369–370. (At the time of writing this paper I was not aware of the disclosures made by Berger.)

2. M. Eliade, *Autobiography II, 1937–1960, Exile's Odyssey* (Chicago: University of Chicago, 1988), ppxiv–xv. In the 1970s he resisted inducements from the Romanian government to return, refusing to make any compromise with the communist dictatorship.

3. Ibid., pp208–9.

4. From M. Eliade, *No Souvenirs* (New York: Harper & Row, 1977), quoted in a review by R.P. Coomaraswamy in *Studies in Comparative Religion*, 12:1–2, 1978, p123.

Eliade, Jung, and ERANOS

Eliade was first invited to the annual ERANOS Conferences in 1950 and attended annually until 1962, the year of Olga Froebe's death, delivering lectures at most conferences. Over the years he met figures like Gershom Scholem, Louis Massignon, Raffael Pettazoni, Joachim Wach, D.T. Suzuki, Guiseppe Tucci, and many others in the ERANOS constellation. In his journal, Eliade recounts his first meeting with Jung at a dinner in an Ascona restaurant:

> [He] is a captivating old gentleman, utterly without conceit, who is as happy to talk as he is to listen. What could I write down here first of this long conversation? Perhaps his bitter reproaches of 'official science'? In university circles he is not taken seriously. 'Scholars have no curiosity,' he says with Anatole France. 'Professors are satisfied with recapitulating what they learned in their youth and what does not cause any trouble....'[1]

In an interview late in his life he again recalled his first meeting with Jung:

> After half an hour's conversation I felt I was listening to a Chinese sage or an east European peasant, still rooted in the Earth Mother yet close to Heaven at the same time. I was enthralled by the wonderful simplicity of his *presence*....[2]

In 1952 Eliade conducted a lengthy interview with Jung for the Parisian magazine *Combat*, at a time when Jung's recently published *Answer to Job* was provoking a stormy controversy.[3] (We

---

1. *Journal 1*, August 23, 1950, quoted in G. Wehr, *Jung, A Biography* (Boston: Shambhala, 1988), pp273–274. In his autobiography, Eliade again refers to Jung's 'bitter comments' about 'official science'. See *Autobiography II*, p147.

2. *Ordeal by Labyrinth*, pp162–3

3. An edited version of this interview can be found in *C.G. Jung Speaking, Interviews and Encounters*, ed. W. McGuire & R.F.C. Hull (London: Thames & Hudson, 1978), pp225–234. Unfortunately Eliade's introductory comments and his interpolations have been severely abridged in this edition.

remember Gershom Scholem's only half-jesting remark that Jung had tried to psychoanalyze Yahweh.)[1] In the same year, Jung read Eliade's book on shamanism and the two had a long and intense conversation about it. They met several times over the next few years, the last occasion being at Kusnacht in 1959 where they had a lengthy conversation in the garden, primarily about the nature of mystical experience. Eliade's rather fragmentary remarks about this last encounter are not without interest. He tells us that Jung no longer had any interest in therapies and case studies, nor in contemporary theology, but that he retained his appetite for patristic theology. He also notes again Jung's disenchantment with the scientific establishment:

> [N]ow and then it seemed to me that I detected a trace of bitterness. Speaking about the structures of mystical experiences, he declared the medical doctors and psychologists are 'too stupid or too uncultivated' to understand such phenomena.[2]

Eliade's connections with the Jungian establishment were institutional as well as personal. In the early 50s, through the influence of Joseph Campbell, he was awarded a special grant by the Bollingen Foundation which enabled him and his wife to escape 'the nightmare of poverty'.[3] Several of Eliade's major works appeared in the Bollingen Series. In 1953 Eliade gave five two-hour lectures at the Jung Institute in Zurich.

There are a great many subjects which commanded the attention of both Jung and Eliade: mythological symbolisms; esoteric spiritual disciplines such as alchemy; the mystical literature of the East; dreams and the structures of the unconscious; the pathologies of modern civilisation, to name a few. One is constantly struck by parallels. For instance, Jung's work on alchemy and Eliade's on shamanism both provided a unified view of reality in which physical and psychic energy are two aspects, or

---

1. *Autobiography II*, p162.
2. Ibid., pp162, 205. See also *No Souvenirs* June 6, 1959, pp41–2.
3. Ibid., p149.

dimensions, of a single reality (hence the possibility of para-normal powers and the like).[1] In their approach to these subjects both showed a sympathetic receptivity to the spiritual messages of the documents they were studying.

There are also obvious parallels in their biographies: academic resistance to their discoveries; the hostility of particular disciplinary coteries (the Freudians in Jung's case, the anthropologists in Eliade's); the importance of ERANOS as a forum where ideas could be ventilated and hypotheses tested amongst kindred spirits; the trips to India, Africa and America; the intrepid exploration of what Eliade calls 'foreign spiritual universes'. Consider this passage from Eliade's journal, written in 1959:

> These thirty years, and more, that I've spent among exotic, barbaric, indomitable gods and goddesses, nourished on myths, obsessed by symbols, nursed and bewitched by so many images which have come down to me from those submerged worlds, today seem to me to be the stages of a long initiation. Each one of these divine figures, each of these myths or symbols, is connected to a danger that was confronted and overcome. How many times I was almost lost, gone astray in this labyrinth where I risked being killed.... These were not only bits of knowledge acquired slowly and leisurely in books, but so many encounters, confrontations, and temptations. I realize perfectly well now all the dangers I skirted during this long quest, and, in the first place, the risk of forgetting that I had a goal...that I wanted to reach a 'center'.[2]

With a few words changed how easily this could have come from Jung! Let me now turn briefly to one of Eliade's main tasks, what he called the 'deprovincialization' of Western culture by a 'creative hermeneutics' which would bring 'foreign spiritual universes' within our purview.

1. G. Wehr, *Jung*, pp254–5.
2. *No Souvenirs*, Nov. 10, 1959, pp74–5.

'Deprovincializing' European
Culture in a 'Crepuscular Era'

In his autobiography Eliade says this:

> [The] re-entry of Asia into history and the discovery of the
> spirituality of archaic societies cannot be without
> consequence.... The camouflage or even occultation of the
> sacred and of spiritual meanings in general characterizes all
> crepuscular eras. It is a matter of the larval survival of the
> original meaning, which in this way becomes *unrecognizable*.
> Hence the importance I ascribe to images, symbols and nar-
> ratives, or more precisely to the hermeneutical analysis
> which describes their meanings and identifies their origi-
> nal functions.[1]

In his ERANOS Lectures in 1953, on earth symbolism in various cultures, Eliade tells us that he

> tried to show the necessity, or rather the obligation, to
> study and understand the spiritual creations of 'primitives'
> with the same zeal and hermeneutical rigor used by West-
> ern elites with respect to their own cultural traditions. I
> was convinced that the documents and method of the his-
> tory of religions lead, more surely than any other historical
> discipline, to the deprovincialization of Western cultures.[2]

There are many parallels here with Jung's work. For the
moment, however, I point out an interesting divergence in their
work. For all his sympathetic inquiries into primal mythologies
and Eastern spirituality, and despite the importance of his
excursions into other cultures, Jung remained resolutely European in his orientation: his intellectual anchorage, so to speak,
was always in the West. This is nicely illustrated by two episodes
from his visit to India: the first is his extraordinary reluctance to

1. *Autobiography II*, p153.
2. Ibid., p166.

visit the great saint and sage of Arunachala, Ramana Maharshi, as if he were either skeptical about the status of Ramana or, more likely, that he felt somewhat threatened by the spiritual force to which such a visit would expose him.[1] Recall also this passage from Jung:

> I had felt the impact of the dreamlike world of India.... My own world of European consciousness had become peculiarly thin, like a network of telegraph wires high above the ground, stretching in straight lines all over the surface of an earth looking treacherously like a geographic globe.

He was profoundly disturbed by the thought that the world of Indian spirituality might be the real world and that the European lived in a 'madhouse of abstractions'.[2] One cannot help but feel that Jung did not fully confront or assimilate this experience, that he turned his back on India in a self-defensive reflex, so to speak.[3] One senses no such inhibition in Eliade's immersion in Indian spirituality: his work ratifies his claim that the three years in India were 'the essential ones in my life. India was my education.'[4]

Let me say a few words about what Eliade defined as his 'essential problems': 'sacred space and time, the structure and function of myth, and the morphology of divine figures.'[5] In Jung's writings, the most common meaning ascribed to 'myth' refers to a personal, inner life, a kind of allegorical narrative

---

1. See C.G. Jung, *Memories*, p 305. Ramana Maharshi is not mentioned by name but is clearly one of the 'holy men' in question. See also T. Burckhardt's comment on this episode in 'Cosmology and Modern Science', in J. Needleman (ed), *The Sword of Gnosis* (Baltimore: Penguin, 1974), p 178. (Burckhardt's essay can also be found in his *Mirror of the Intellect* [Cambridge: Quinta Essentia, 1987].)

2. Quoted in G. Wehr, *Jung*, p 283

3. Jung has been similarly criticized for his limited understanding of Chinese spirituality. One is reminded of the somewhat unkind joke, 'What is Chinese philosophy? Well, there is *yin*, and *yang*, and then there is Jung.'

4. *Ordeal by Labyrinth*, p 54.

5. *Autobiography II*, p 174.

embedded deep in the psyche. Nevertheless, Jung is sometimes prepared to go beyond purely psychic understandings of myth. One remembers the vivid account in his autobiography of his encounter with the Taos Pueblo Indians in 1925, and in particular, the meeting with an Indian elder named Ochwiay Biano. The elder was bewildered by the attempts of the American authorities to curtail Indian ritual life. The Indians, he claimed, performed an indispensable service for all Americans, and indeed all peoples:

> After all, we are a people who live on the roof of the world; we are the sons of Father Sun, and with our religion we daily help our father to go across the sky. We do this not only for ourselves, but for the whole world. If we were to cease practicing our religion, in ten years the sun would no longer rise. Then it would be night forever.[1]

Jung's commentary on this:

> If for a moment we put away all European rationalism and transport ourselves into the clear mountain air of that solitary plateau ... if we also set aside our intimate knowledge of the world and exchange it for a horizon which seems immeasurable ... we will begin to achieve an inner comprehension of the Pueblo Indian's point of view.... That man feels capable of formulating valid replies to the overpowering influence of God, and that he can render back something which is essential even to God, induces pride, for it raises the human individual to the dignity of a metaphysical factor.[2]

Jung also remarks on the way in which our scientific knowledge impoverishes rather than enriches us by cutting us from the mythic world. This anticipates in striking fashion one of the most persistent motifs in Eliade's work on archaic cultures: the

---

1. *Memories*, p280.
2. Ibid., p281.

theme of archaic ontology and cosmic responsibility. Jung's insight into the 'cosmic meaning of consciousness' was reinforced during his visit to the Athi Plains near Nairobi, where he more clearly understood man's responsibility as a 'second creator', again a theme which Eliade has pursued indefatigably.[1]

Jung's insights into archaic mythologies and cosmologies was undoubtedly of decisive importance in Eliade's intellectual development. Clearly Eliade, like Joseph Campbell, was influenced by Jung's work which disclosed what he called a 'universal parallelism' of analogous symbolisms and motifs in mythologies from all over the world.[2] Eliade repeatedly acknowledges the debt. At points Jung concedes the metaphysical status of myths:

> No science will ever replace myth, and a myth cannot be made out of any science. For it is not that 'God' is a myth, but that myth is the revelation of a divine life in man. It is not we who invent myth, rather it speaks to us as a Word of God.[3]

But one finds in Jung the more or less constant attempt to bring archaic cosmology and metaphysics back into the psychic domain while Eliade is prepared to go beyond it. This can be seen in the different senses in which Jung and Eliade use the term 'archetypes': for Jung the archetypes are 'structures of the collective unconscious' while Eliade uses the term in its neo-Platonic sense of exemplary and 'transhistorical' paradigms.[4] Jung also tended to homologize dreams and myths. In this context, Eliade's differentiation of the two is suggestive:

> The resemblances between dreams and myths are obvious, but the difference between them is an essential one: there is the same gulf between the two as between an act of

---

1. Ibid., p284.
2. See A. Jaffé, *The Myth of Meaning* (Baltimore: Penguin, 1975), p15.
3. Ibid., p373.
4. *Autobiography II*, p162.

adultery and *Madame Bovary*; that is, between a simple experience and a creation of the human spirit.[1]

Likewise Jung's interest in the qualitative determinations of time, most notably in his ideas about synchronicity and psychosynthesis,[2] remains within the psychic arena while for Eliade sacred time is itself an irreducible category and one altogether indispensable to an understanding of the archaic and mythological modes.[3] Jung evinced much less interest in the question of sacred space which has been one of Eliade's preoccupations.

The bringing of other spiritual universes within the ambit of the West was an important but subsidiary task in Jung's life-work; it was the motive force in Eliade's work. The following passage from *Myths, Dreams and Mysteries* might well stand as a epigraph for Eliade's work over half a century:

> the 'exotic' and 'primitive' peoples have now come within the orbit of history, so that Western man is obliged to enquire into their systems of values if he is to be able to establish and maintain communication with them.... We have to approach the symbols, myths and rites of the Oceanians or the Africans ... with the same respect and the same desire to learn that we have devoted to Western cultural creations, even when those rites and myths reveal 'strange', terrible or aberrant aspects.[4]

Clearly, for Eliade this was not simply a grandiose academic project but one driven by certain existential imperatives, as was the case with Jung's studies. Consider this, for instance, from Eliade's *Journal*:

---

1. *Ordeal by Labyrinth*, p162. (Clearly this formulation, a characteristic one, is open to the charge that it reduces myths to no more than cultural creations.)

2. See *Memories*, p160 & G. Wehr, *Jung*, p111.

3. Eliade's most accessible treatment of this theme is to be found in *The Sacred and the Profane* (New York: Harcourt Brace Jovanovich, 1957).

4. M. Eliade, *Myths, Dreams and Mysteries* (New York: Harper & Row, 1960), pp9, 10, 12.

it is not some kind of infatuation with the past that makes me want to go back to the world of the Australian aborigines or the Eskimos. I want to recognize myself—in the philosophical sense—in my fellow men.[1]

Eliade discerns a great divide in the human past, cutting off archaic and historical man from modern man. Archaic man lives in a world whose meaning and value is articulated symbolically, through a mythology which is re-actualized in ritual and ceremonial life. Historical man is more conscious of himself in time but his world view remains profoundly religious and spiritual. Modern man, by contrast, lives not in an ordered and meaningful cosmos but a chaotic, opaque, and mute universe in which he has lost the capacity for religious experience: 'the desacralized cosmos is a recent discovery of the human spirit.'[2] Such is the legacy of a materialistic scientism. These differences are thrown into sharp relief in Eliade's work by his treatment of archaic and modern ways of understanding time and space.

For the traditional mentality space is not homogeneous, as it is for modern science, but is qualitatively determined. Sacred space, both natural and man-made, is ordered, meaningful and centered, while profane space is chaotic, meaningless and threatening. Sacred space is 'organized' round a centre, a point at which hierophanies occur, at which the barriers between the physical, psychic and spiritual dimensions of reality become permeable and transparent. Time too is *qualitatively* determined, and is cyclical and repeatable, or 'recoverable'. Space and time are sanctified by their relationship to that which is sacred, which is to say that which is immutable, beyond the world of flux, beyond time and space. Modern conceptions of time and space, on the other hand, are mechanistic, materialistic and one-dimensional. Furthermore, says Eliade, our encounters with other spiritual universes are urgently necessary for our own spiritual health. We must no longer regard them as immature

1. *Ordeal by Labyrinth*, p137.
2. *The Sacred and the Profane*, p13.

episodes or as aberrations from some exemplary history of man—a history conceived, of course, only as that of Western man.'[1]

Science, Religion, and Personal Faith

I move now to the most problematic part of this paper, a consideration of the place of science, religion and personal faith in the work of Jung and Eliade. Shortly before their falling-out, Freud made the following plea to Jung:

> My dear Jung, promise me never to abandon the sexual theory. That is the most essential thing of all. You see, we must make of it an unshakable bulwark.

To Jung's somewhat astonished query as to what this bulwark must stand against, Freud replied, 'Against the black tide of the mud . . . of occultism.' In *Memories, Dreams, Reflections* Jung makes this comment:

> Freud, who had always made much of his irreligiosity, had constructed a dogma; or rather, in the place of a jealous God whom he had lost, he had substituted another compelling image, that of sexuality . . . the 'sexual libido' took over the role of a *deus absconditus*, a hidden or concealed god. . . . The advantage of this transformation for Freud was, apparently, that he was able to regard the new numinous principle as scientifically irreproachable and free from all religious taint. At bottom, however, the numinosity, that is, the psychological qualities of the two rationally incommensurable opposites—Yahweh and sexuality—remained the same . . . the lost god now had to be sought below, not above.[2]

---

1. M. Eliade, *Australian Religions* (Ithaca: Cornell University, 1971), pxix.
2. *Memories*, pp174–5. To this passage Jung adds this astounding remark, 'But what difference does it make, ultimately, to the stronger agency if it is called now by one name, and now by another?' (Jung seems impervious to the very great difference made by these respective angles of approach, so to speak.)

Soon after the breakdown of their relationship Freud spoke disparagingly of Jung's 'disregard for scientific logic'[1] to which Jung might well have replied with the maxim we find in *Memories*: 'Overvalued reason has this in common with political absolutism: under its dominion the individual is pauperized.'[2] The episode raises several interesting questions about the way Freud, Jung and Eliade positioned themselves in relation to the ideology of modern science and to religion.

For Freud psychoanalysis was a rigorously scientific discipline which must remain uncontaminated by all those modes of understanding which he herded together under the pejorative label of 'occultism'. Freud's views on religion are well known and need not be rehearsed here; as Jung noted in *Memories* Freud saw any expression of spirituality as a function of repressed sexuality.[3] Suffice it to say that Freud surrendered to a severely reductionist view altogether characteristic of the late nineteenth intellectual alienated from religious tradition.[4] For Jung the problem was much more complex. He rejected the narrow dogmatism and stifling moralism which characterized his father's faith but affirmed the richness, potency and psychologically liberating elements within Christianity and in esoteric Western traditions such as gnosticism, hermeticism, and alchemy:

all religions [wrote Jung], down to the forms of magical religion of primitives, are psychotherapies, which treat and

1. See G. Wehr, *Jung*, p 22.
2. *Memories*, p 333.
3. Ibid., p 172.
4. For a brief but useful account of Freud's views on religion see D.W.D. Shaw, *The Dissuaders* (London: SCM, 1978). In his *Journal* Eliade dismisses Freud's extraordinary lucubrations on this subject thus: his 'explanations of religious experiences and other spiritual activities are purely and simply inept'. *Journal 1* April 23, 1953, quoted in G. Steiner, 'Ecstasies, not arguments', review article on Eliade's *Journals*, in *Times Literary Supplement* September 28–October 4, 1990, p 1015. For an interesting account of the effects of Freud's alienation from his Judaic heritage, see W. Perry, *Challenges to a Secular Society* (Oakton: Foundation for Traditional Studies, 1996), pp 17–38.

heal the sufferings of the soul, and those of the body that come from the soul.[1]

On the other side, Jung rejected the materialism of a profane science whilst retaining his faith in an empirical mode of inquiry. The appeal of psychiatry, he tells us, was precisely that it was a meeting ground for the biological and the spiritual:

> Here was the empirical field common to biological and spiritual facts, which I had everywhere sought and nowhere found. Here at last was the place where the collision of nature and spirit became a reality.[2]

This, of course, anticipates the great Jungian theme of *coincidentia oppositorum*, the reconciliation of opposites.

In Eliade's work, the opposites present themselves not as the 'biological' and the 'spiritual' but rather in terms of a set of dichotomies which structure the whole of his agenda: the sacred and the profane; the archaic and the modern; the mythological and the historical; the poetic and the scientific. Eliade's work as a whole can be seen as a project to recuperate the former mode of each of these pairings. For Eliade the problem of scientific materialism exerted itself largely through the reductionist models of the anthropologists. Eliade's task was to 'revalorize' manifestations of the sacred, to restore to them their experiential and ontological meanings and to resist the 'audacious and irrelevant interpretations' of reductionists of every ilk—Marxist, Freudian, Durkheimian, or whatever.[3]

> Such a demystifying attitude [he wrote] ought to be arraigned in its turn, on charges of ethnocentrism, of Western provincialism', and so, ultimately, be demystified itself.[4]

---

1. A 1935 paper on psychotherapy, quoted in G. Wehr, *Jung*, p293.
2. *Memories*, p130.
3. M. Eliade *The Quest, History and Meaning in Religion* (Chicago: University of Chicago, 1969), p5.
4. *Ordeal by Labyrinth*, p137.

Eliade also challenged his own colleagues:

the majority of the historians of religion defend themselves against the messages with which their documents are filled. This caution is understandable. One does not live with impunity in intimacy with 'foreign' religious forms.... But many historians of religion end by no longer taking seriously the spiritual worlds they study; they fall back on their personal religious faith, or they take refuge in a materialism or behaviorism impervious to every spiritual shock.[1]

One of Eliade's most important contributions to the discipline of religious studies was his insistence on explanatory categories which are *sui generis*, peculiar to religious phenomena, which are autonomous, so to speak. Here Eliade is much closer to the great German theologian, Rudolf Otto:

a religious phenomenon will only be recognized as such if it is grasped at its own level, that is to say, if it is studied as something religious. To try to grasp the essence of such a phenomenon by means of physiology, psychology, sociology, economics, linguistics, art, or any other study is false; it misses the one unique and irreducible element in it—the element of the sacred. Obviously there are no purely religious phenomena.... But it would be hopeless to try and explain religion in terms of any one of these basic functions.... It would be as futile as thinking you could explain *Madame Bovary* by a list of social, economic and political facts; however true, they do not effect it as a work of literature.[2]

One cannot help noticing in the autobiographical writings of both Jung and Eliade a certain reticence about their own religious beliefs and affiliations. Eliade remarked, in an interview

1. *The Quest*, p 62.
2. M. Eliade, *Patterns in Comparative Religion* (New York: Sheed & Ward, 1958), p xiii. Eliade acknowledges his debt to Otto in the opening pages of *The Sacred and the Profane*.

late in his life, 'I made the decision long ago to maintain a kind of discreet silence as to what I personally believe or don't believe.'[1] One obvious possibility is that both felt that too open an affirmation of such beliefs might compromise their academic standing in a milieu which privileged the ideal of a scientific objectivity and detachment, to such an extent, indeed, that one can speak here of a kind of pseudo-cult. Professional pressures and expectations sometimes 'diluted [Jung's] most potent observations in deference to a more conventional audience.'[2] As Jung himself observed in a frequently cited passage, 'Today the voice of one crying in the wilderness must necessarily strike a scientific tone if the ear of the multitude is to be reached.'[3]

Another possibility is that both struggled with the problems of religious faith without ever resolving the many difficult questions which were latent in Nietzsche's famous pronouncement of 'the death of God'. We remember the inscription over the doorway at Kusnacht, the maxim which Jung found in the writings of Erasmus: 'Invoked or not, the god will be present.' Jung himself said of this inscription:

> It is a Delphic oracle though. It says: yes, the god will be on the spot, but in what form and to what purpose? I have put the inscription there to remind my patients and myself: *timor dei initium sapientiae* ('The fear of the Lord is the beginning of wisdom.' Psalm 11:10)[4]

Remember also remember Jung's famous remark, in an interview in 1955, that

> All that I have learned has led me step by step to an unshakable conviction of the existence of God. I only believe in

1. *Ordeal by Labyrinth*, p132.
2. P. Novak, 'C.G. Jung in the light of Asian Psychology', *Religious Traditions*, 14, 1991, pp66–7.
3. Quoted in Wolfgang Smith, *Cosmos and Transcendence* (San Rafael, CA: Sophia Perennis, 2008), pp114–115.
4. Letter, quoted in G. Wehr, *Jung*, p93.

what I know. And that eliminates believing. Therefore I do not take His existence on belief—I *know* that He exists.[1]

There seems no doubt that Jung underwent an experience of a transcendent reality: in later life, he tells us, he became almost exclusively concerned with those events and happenings where the 'imperishable world irrupted into the transitory one.'[2] The problem remained: how to describe, define, conceptualize this experience and what place to give it in his professional work? The problem for us is how, precisely, we are to understand Jung's somewhat contradictory writings about the exact nature and status of the realities he understood to be signalled by terms like 'archetype', 'collective unconscious', and, perhaps most vexingly, 'God'. Gerhard Wehr, one of Jung's several biographers, claims that

> In Jung, as in no other psychologist of his time, the superindividual was paramount. A decisive role was played by the transpersonal, not only as a biologically and instinctually grounded driving force, but as an 'archetype', a physical, mental, and spiritual motive power that points beyond man precisely by engaging him in a lifelong process of maturation.[3]

This kind of formulation, it seems to me, wants to have it every which way: the 'superindividual' is subsumed in the term 'archetype' which then becomes, simultaneously, 'a physical, mental and spiritual motive force.' This, to say the least of it, amounts to hedging one's bets!

1. 'Men, Women and God', interviews with Frederick Sands, in *C.G. Jung Speaking*, p 251. Cf., 'I find that all my thoughts circle around God like the planets round the sun, and are as irresistibly attracted by Him. I would feel it to be the grossest sin if I were to oppose any resistance to this force.' Letter to a young clergyman, quoted in Aniela Jaffé's Introduction to *Memories*, p13.
2. G. Wehr, *Jung*, p23.
3. Ibid., p4.

The Perennialist Critique
of Jung and Eliade

Jung's work was attacked from the scientific side as being 'symbolistic', 'mystical', 'occultist', and the like, just as Eliade's work in turn has been attacked as 'Jungian' and 'Catholic', lacking in 'objectivity' and motivated by 'unscientific zeal'.[1] These kinds of criticisms are of no interest in the present context. Much more disturbing, from my point of view, are the charges that have been pressed by exponents of the traditional religious outlook. The most incisive of these critics are perennialists such as René Guénon, Ananda Coomaraswamy, Frithjof Schuon, and Titus Burckhardt. I do not have time here to rehearse the premises from which such thinkers start—we may turn to this in the discussion later. Let us look briefly at a few of the criticisms that have been made. There are four kinds of criticisms which deserve our attention. I shall flag these criticisms by identifying their targets: pan-psychism; the denial of metaphysics; the tyranny of the ego; the repudiation of traditional religion.

From a traditionalist perspective the first problem is that Jung's writings often seem to confound the psychic and the spiritual. In Jung's case it is a matter at times of reducing the spiritual to the level of the psychic (a form of psychologism), and at others of elevating the psychic to the level of the spiritual, or, to put the same point differently, of deifying the unconscious.[2] In *Memories* Jung states that

All comprehension and all that is comprehended is in itself psychic, and to that extent we are hopelessly cooped up in an exclusively psychic world.[3]

---

1. See, for example, Edmund Leach's smug review article, 'Sermons from a Man on a Ladder', *New York Review of Books*, Oct. 20, 1966, pp28–31.

2. See R. Guénon, 'The Confusion of the Psychic and the Spiritual' and 'The Misdeeds of Psychoanalysis', in *The Reign of Quantity and the Signs of the Times* (Hillsdale, NY: Sophia Perennis, 2004).

3. *Memories*, p385.

It is difficult to find in Jung's writings a completely unequivocal affirmation of the objective and supra-psychic reality of the
numen, to borrow a term from Otto, a figure who significantly
influenced both Jung and Eliade.[1] In the interview conducted by
Eliade for *Combat*, Jung *does* say this:

> Religious experience is numinous, as Rudolf Otto calls it,
> and for me, as a psychologist, this experience differs from
> all others in the way it transcends the ordinary categories
> of time, space and causality.[2]

However, many of his formulations on this subject are ambivalent. It is also undoubtedly true that a great many people,
including Christian theologians, have used Jung's sometimes
confusing ruminations as a theoretical platform for a wholesale
psychologizing of religion—Don Cuppitt, to name but one popular exponent of the absurd view that religion needs no metaphysical underpinnings.[3] This is to be guilty of what Frithjof
Schuon has called the 'psychological imposture' which he casti-
gates in these terms:

> the tendency to reduce everything to psychological factors
> and to call into question not only what is intellectual and
> spiritual ... but also the human spirit as such, and therewith

1. The same kind of ambivalence is evident in most Jungian formulations
concerning both the collective unconscious and archetypes. This, for instance,
from Marie-Louise von Franz: 'Really, it is a modern, scientific expression for an
inner experience that has been known to mankind from time immemorial, the
experience in which strange and unknown things from our own inner world
happen to us, in which influences from within can suddenly alter us, in which
we have dreams and ideas which we feel as if we are not doing ourselves, but
which appear in us strangely and overwhelmingly. In earlier times these influences were attributed to a divine fluid (mana), or to a god, demon, or 'spirit', a fitting expression of the feeling that this influence has an objective, quite foreign
and autonomous existence, as well as the sense of its being something overpowering, which has the conscious ego at its mercy'; per G. Wehr, *Jung*, p170.

2. *C. G. Jung Speaking*, p230 (italics mine).

3. See the glib commentary by Cuppitt on Jung's view of 'religion', quoted
in S. Segaller & M. Berger, *Jung, The Wisdom of the Dream* (Chatswood: Peribo,
1989), p179.

its capacity of adequation and still more evidently, its inward illimitation and transcendence. . . . Psychoanalysis is at once an endpoint and a cause, as is always the case with profane ideologies, like materialism and evolutionism, of which it is really a logical and fateful ramification and a natural ally.[1]

Schuon's reference to materialism and evolutionism alert us to these two 19th century bugbears (still very much with us, alas!) which occasionally raise their ugly heads in Jung's writings. Even in the autobiography written near the end of his life, Jung is capable of a kind of scientistic gobbledygook which betrays a failure to break free from the stultifying effects of these prejudices. Two examples: 'Consciousness is phylogenetically and ontogenetically a secondary phenomenon.'[2] (This is a variant on the preposterous evolutionist inversion whereby 'flesh' becomes 'word'.) Likewise in his Introduction to *The Secret of the Golden Flower*, Jung descends into Darwinian hocus-pocus when he suggests that the analogical relationships of symbolic vocabularies and mythological motifs across many different cultures derives from 'the identity of cerebral structures beyond all racial differences'.[3] Here the psychic domain seems to have itself been reduced to nothing more than an epiphenomenon of a material substrate. This is Jung at his worst, surrendering to a materialistic scientism which he elsewhere disavows.

1. F. Schuon, *Survey of Metaphysics and Esoterism* (Bloomington: World Wisdom, 1986), p195.

2. *Memories*, p381.

3. From Jung's Introduction to *The Secret of the Golden Flower*, quoted by Burckhardt in 'Cosmology and Modern Science', p168. The traditionalist critique of Jung's thought cannot be canvassed in any detail here, though some of the comments made in this discussion clearly draw on traditionalist understandings. See also P. Sherrard, 'An Introduction to the Religious Thought of C.J. Jung', *Studies in Comparative Religion*, 3:1, 1969; W. Smith, *Cosmos and Transcendence*, chap. 6; and W. Perry, *The Widening Breach: Evolutionism in the Mirror of Cosmology* (Cambridge: Quinta Essentia, 1995), p89. Sherrard argues that Jung's thought can best be understood as an agenda for the displacement of Christianity while Smith highlights some of the contradictions and the 'dogmatic relativism' which betrays Jung's confusion of the spiritual with the psychic. Perry notes how Jung inverts the traditional doctrine of Archetypes.

In *Psychology and Religion* Jung staked out his most characteristic position on metaphysics:

> Psychology treats ... all metaphysical ... assertions as mental phenomena, and regards them as statements about the mind and its structure that derive ultimately from certain unconscious dispositions. It does not consider them to be absolutely valid or even capable of establishing metaphysical truth. ... Psychology therefore holds that the mind cannot establish or assert anything beyond itself.[1]

In similar vein, this:

> I am and remain a psychologist. I am not interested in anything that transcends the psychological content of human experience. I do not even ask myself whether such transcendence is possible. ...[2]

Jung, to his credit, was not always able to hold fast to this position. In 1946, for example, he was prepared to write that 'archetypes ... have a nature that cannot with certainty be designated as psychic', and that the archetype is a 'metaphysical' entity not susceptible to any unequivocal (i.e., 'scientific') definition.[3] The 'status' of archetypes is a critical issue, particularly if we take the following kind of claim seriously: 'The basis of analytical psychology's significance for the psychology of religion ... lies in C.G. Jung's discovery of how archetypal images, events and experiences, individually and in groups, are the *essential* determinants of the *religious* life in history and in the present.'[4]

From a traditional point of view there are two problems: the first is the suggestion, not hard to find in Jung's writings, that the psychic domain contains and exhausts all of supra-material reality, a view we have already designated pan-psychism. But even

---

1. 'Psychology and Religion', quoted in P. Novak, 'C.G. Jung in the light of Asian Psychology', p68.
2. Interview with Eliade for *Combat*, in *C.G. Jung Speaking*, p229.
3. 'On the Nature of the Psyche', quoted in A. Jaffé, *The Myth of Meaning*, p23.
4. G. Wehr, *Jung*, p291 (italics mine).

when Jung retreats from this position (as in the passage just cited), he still insists that the psychic is the only supra-material reality that we can explore and *know*. From the viewpoint of traditional metaphysics this amounts to nothing less than a denial of the Intellect, that faculty by which Absolute Reality can be apprehended, and to which all traditional wisdoms testify.[1]

What of 'God'? Jung's position, at least as Aniela Jaffé recalls it, is subtle but clear: 'God' and 'the unconscious' are inseparable from the point of view of the subject but not identical. One of Jung's most careful formulations on the subject goes like this:

> This is certainly not to say that what we call the unconscious is identical with God or set up in his place. It is simply the medium from which religious experience seems to flow.

So far so good. The problem arises in what follows: 'As to what the further cause of such experience may be, the answer to this lies beyond the range of human knowledge.'[2] Elsewhere he affirmed that, 'the transcendental reality...[beyond] the world inside and outside ourselves...is as certain as our own existence.'[3] Nevertheless, it *necessarily* remains an unfathomable mystery. In denying the possibility of intellection and of absolute certitude concerning metaphysical realities Jung again falls foul of the traditionalists. Compare Jung's notion that we 'are hopelessly cooped up in an exclusively psychic world' and that the cause of religious experience 'lies beyond human knowledge' with this kind of claim from Frithjof Schuon:

> The distinctive mark of man is total intelligence, that is to say an intelligence which is objective and capable of con-

1. See P. Novak, 'C.G. Jung in the light of Asian Psychology', p77. At other points Jung's philosophical position is also reminiscent of a kind of 'existentialist' relativism. Thus, 'the sole purpose of human existence is to kindle a light in the darkness of mere being'; *Memories*, p358.

2. From 'The Undiscovered Self', in *Civilisation in Transition*, quoted in A. Jaffé, *The Myth of Meaning*, p40.

3. From *Mysterium Coniunctionis*, quoted in A. Jaffé, *The Myth of Meaning*, p42.

ceiving the absolute.... This objectivity...would lack any sufficient reason did it not have the capacity to conceive the absolute or infinite....[1]

Or, even more succinctly,

The prerogative of the human state is objectivity, the essential content of which is the Absolute. There is no knowledge without objectivity of the intelligence....[2]

Furthermore,

This capacity for objectivity and absoluteness is an anticipated and existential refutation of all the ideologies of doubt: if man is able to doubt, this is because certitude exists; likewise the very notion of illusion proves that man has access to reality.[3]

Another stumbling block concerns the relationship of the empirical ego and consciousness. Ananda Coomaraswamy signals the problem when he writes,

The health envisaged by empirical psychotherapy is a freedom from *particular* pathogenic conditions; that envisaged by sacred or traditional psychology is freedom from *all* conditions and predicaments.[4]

In other words, Jung sought to rehabilitate the empirical ego rather than to dismantle it. From a traditionalist point of view Jung hoists himself on his own petard when he writes 'To us consciousness is inconceivable without an ego.... I cannot

1. F. Schuon, 'To be Man is to Know', *Studies in Comparative Religion*, 13:1–2, 1979, pp117–118.
2. F. Schuon, *Esoterism as Principle and as Way* (Bloomington: World Wisdom, 1981), p15ff.
3. F. Schuon, *Logic and Transcendence* (New York: Harper & Row, 1975), p13.
4. A.K. Coomaraswamy, 'On the Indian and Traditional Psychology, or rather, Pneumatology', in *Coomaraswamy, vol. 2, Selected Papers: Metaphysics* (Princeton: Princeton University, 1977), p335 (italics mine). See also T. Burckhardt, 'Cosmology and Modern Science', pp174–175.

imagine a conscious mental state that does not relate to the ego. . . .'[1] Daniel Goleman elaborates the crucial point:

> The models of contemporary psychology . . . foreclose the acknowledgement or investigation of a mode of being which is the central premise and *summum bonum* of virtually every Eastern psycho-spiritual system. Called variously Enlightenment, Buddhahood . . . and so on, there is simply no fully equivalent category in contemporary psychology.[2]

Fourthly, several traditionalists, most notably Philip Sherrard, have argued that Jung's covert and perhaps not fully conscious agenda was nothing less than the dethronement of Christianity in all of its traditional and institutional forms, and its replacement by a kind of quasi-religious psychology for which Jung himself was a 'prophetic' voice. A variant of this particular kind of argument has been elaborated by Philip Rieff and is adumbrated in the following passage:

> After the failure of the Reformation, and the further fragmentation of Christianity, the search was on for those more purely symbolical authorities to which an educated Christian could transfer his loyalty from the Church. Biblicism gave way to erudition, erudition to historical liberalism, and the latter to a variety of psychological conservatisms, of which Jung's is potentially the most attractive for those not entirely unchurched.[3]

---

1. From 'Psychology and Religion', quoted by P. Novak, 'C.G. Jung in the light of Asian Psychology', p82.

2. Quoted in P. Novak, 'C.G. Jung in the light of Asian Psychology', p73. As Goleman goes on to say, 'The paradigms of traditional Asian psychologies, however, are capable of encompassing the major categories of contemporary psychology as well as this other mode of consciousness.' One again sees the problem in Jung's homologizing of the psychosis of the mental patient with the 'mythopoeic imagination which has vanished from our rational age'; *Memories*, p213.

3. P. Rieff, *The Triumph of the Therapeutic* (Harmondsworth: Penguin, 1973), p110.

This kind of argument would seem to have some cogency when we recall some of Jung's many explanations of his own relationship to religion. Take this, for example, from a letter written in 1946:

> I practice science, not apologetics and not philosophy.... My interest is a scientific one.... I proceed from a positive Christianity that is as much Catholic as Protestant, and my concern is to point out in a scientifically responsible way those empirically tangible facts which would at least make plausible the legitimacy of Christian and especially Catholic dogma.[1]

The traditionalist response to this kind of claim is quite implacable. Thus Schuon:

> Modern science ... can neither add nor subtract anything in respect of the total truth or of mythological or other symbolism or in respect of the principles and experiences of the spiritual life.... We cannot be too wary of all these attempts to reduce the values vehicled by tradition to the level of phenomena supposed to be scientifically controllable. The spirit escapes the hold of profane science in an absolute fashion.[2]

In the light of these kinds of criticisms it is not hard to see why one traditionalist has suggested that, 'In the final analysis, what Jung has to offer is a religion for atheists ...'[3] or why Rieff claims that Jung's thought amounts to 'a religion for heretics'.[4] In a wonderfully ambiguous phrase, a Dominican admirer of Jung called him 'a priest without a surplice.'[5] It was meant as a compliment but if we take the lack of a surplice as signifying Jung's detachment from any religious tradition then the epithet

---

1. Quoted in G. Wehr, *Jung*, p302.
2. F. Schuon, 'No Activity Without Truth', in *The Sword of Gnosis*, pp36–37.
3. W. Smith, *Cosmos and Transcendence*, p135.
4. P. Rieff, *The Triumph of the Therapeutic*, p115.
5. W. Smith, *Cosmos and Transcendence*, p138.

carries a different freight.[1] (To make the same point differently, 'a priest without a surplice' is no priest at all.)

On theological questions Mircea Eliade often retreats into a post-Nietzschean kind of *credo*. In 1965, for example, he wrote this:

> In a 'world' composed of billions of galaxies... all the classical arguments for or against the existence of God seem to me naive and even childish. I do not think that, for the moment, we have the right to argue philosophically. The problem itself should be left in suspension as it is. We must content ourselves with personal certitudes, with wagers based on dreams, with divinations, ecstasies, aesthetic emotion. That also is a mode of knowing, but without arguments....[2]

Eliade only reveals something of his personal religious beliefs in informal mode in his autobiographical writings, almost, one feels, when he is caught off guard. Like Jung he was often prepared to state things more directly face to face than he was in more professional contexts. In an interview with Claude-Henri Rocquet, Eliade put the matter quite unequivocally:

> If God doesn't exist, then everything is dust and ashes. If there is no absolute to give meaning and value to our existence, then that means that existence has no meaning. I know there are philosophers who do think precisely that; but for me, that would be not just pure despair but also a kind of betrayal. Because it isn't true, and I know that it isn't true.[3]

---

1. Since this paper was written, Steven Wasserstrom has produced a major study exploring this theme, *Religion After Religion: Gershom Scholem, Mircea Eliade and Henry Corbin at Eranos* (Princeton: Princeton University, 1999). See also chap. 5 of my *Journeys East*.

2. *Journal II*, quoted in G. Steiner, 'Ecstasies, not arguments', p1015.

3. *Ordeal by Labyrinth*, p67.

However, Eliade's apparent lack of any personal commitment to a religious tradition and his failure to understand the full implications of the many scriptures and sacred writings in which he immersed himself have been trenchantly criticized by traditionalists. David Lake: 'One has the impression of an uprooted and genial academic busily drifting from article to article, without inward centre or the intellectual discrimination to master his prodigious mental fertility.'[1] Rama Coomaraswamy is even harsher: 'The man is a dilettante, a mere scholar, and in outlook, a totally profane person. When I say he is a dilettante, I refer to the spiritual realm.'[2] Both reviewers accuse Eliade of a kind of psychologism but take no account of Eliade's own exposure of psychological relativism. In *No Souvenirs*, for instance (the book under review by both Coomaraswamy and Lake) Eliade has this to say:

> Psychoanalysis justifies its importance by asserting that it forces you to look to and accept reality. But what sort of reality? A reality conditioned by the materialistic and scientific ideology of psychoanalysis, that is, a historical product....[3]

Jung and Eliade in Perspective

Where does all this leave us? Considered from the perennialist perspective both Jung and Eliade can be accused of a kind of 'humanism' with quasi-religious trappings; from this point of view they are implicated in the destruction of religion begun by the materialistic and humanistic sciences of the Renaissance and more or less completed by Darwinian evolutionism and Freudian psychoanalysis. As Ananda Coomaraswamy so neatly put it, 'While nineteenth century materialism closed the mind

1. D. Lake, review of *No Souvenirs* in *Studies in Comparative Religion*, 13:3–4, 1978, p244.

2. R.P. Coomaraswamy, Review of *No Souvenirs* in *Studies in Comparative Religion*, 13:1–2, 1978, p123.

3. *No Souvenirs*, Oct. 7, 1965, p269.

of man to what is above him, twentieth century psychology opened it to what is below him.'[1]

Certainly I cannot accept either Jung or Eliade as sages or prophets: they both exemplify some of the confusions of the age in their life and work. I am not much impressed by the 'prophetic' tone which each sometimes strikes in writing of their own work. Our age has not been much blessed by either sages or prophets, and it is perhaps not surprising that both Jung and Eliade have sometimes been mistaken for such. The fact that they cannot live up to the claims of their more extravagant admirers is no reason to dismiss or ignore their work which has a richness and depth not often found amongst the self-styled savants of our times. Both Jung and Eliade were profoundly concerned with man's position in a world in which science had stripped the cosmos of meaning, apparently eroded the pillars of religious faith, and robbed man of his spiritual dignity. Whatever our views on some of the questions I have been canvassing, we should be grateful to both Jung and Eliade for rescuing their respective disciplines from the clutches of the materialists and their accomplices, and for their attempts to bridge the apparent chasm between traditional religion and modern science. Nevertheless, if we are to draw what is valuable from their work we need to maintain a sense of proportion and to apply a discernment which, I believe, can only be drawn from the treasuries of metaphysical and spiritual teachings found within each of the integral religious traditions. As for Jung, I cannot improve on Philip Novak's carefully considered judgement:

> Of Jung's enduring value, however, there can be no doubt. For modern psychotherapy and the religious quest alike, he dug a seed-bed from which much life-giving and soul-invigorating insight has sprung.... But Jung yearned for absoluteness and for Truth—he so wanted to bring a saving message to man—and the clash of this yearning with his

---

1. A.K. Coomaraswamy, quoted in W. Perry, 'Drug-Induced Mysticism', *Tomorrow*, 12:2, 1964, p196. (Coomaraswamy was paraphrasing René Guénon.)

avowed vocation, that of empirical scientist and physician, created a lifelong battle of forces within his breast. These tensions spilled over to the printed page, not least when Jung had there to confront the Asian systems which adumbrated the spiritual completion of psychological man that he sought, but with doctrines and methods he could not accept.[1]

The more crucial general point towards which Novak's assessment points is one which the twentieth century is determined to ignore. It has been precisely stated by Frithjof Schuon:

> Outside tradition there can assuredly be found some relative truths or views of partial realities, but outside tradition there does not exist a doctrine that catalyzes absolute truth and transmits liberating notions concerning total reality.[2]

---

1. P. Novak, 'Jung in the light of Asian Psychology', p84.

2. F. Schuon, 'No Activity Without Truth', p36. To this might be added another passage of the most far-reaching significance (from the same essay): 'Nothing is more misleading than to pretend, as is so glibly done in our day, that the religions have compromised themselves hopelessly in the course of the centuries or that they are now played out. If one knows what a religion really consists of, one also knows that the religions cannot compromise themselves and that they are independent of human doings... tradition, let it be repeated, cannot 'become bankrupt', rather it is of the bankruptcy of man that one should speak, for it is he who that has lost all intuition of the supernatural. It is man who has let himself be deceived by the discoveries and inventions of a falsely totalitarian science'; p29.

Allen Ginsberg, a Buddhist Beat

What we [the Beats] were proposing was some new sense of spiritual consciousness. We were interested in non-violence, sexual freedom, the exploration of psychedelic drugs and sensitivity. We were aware that the entire government . . . was corrupt. We were interested in Eastern thought and meditation. We had quite an open heart and open mind. . . .[1]

Allen Ginsberg

Every era has to reinvent the project of 'spirituality' for itself. . . . In the modern era one of the most active metaphors for the spiritual project is 'art' . . . a particularly adaptable site on which to stage the formal dramas besetting consciousness, each individual work of art being a more or less astute paradigm for regulating or reconciling these contradictions. . . .[2]

Susan Sontag

Introduction

On May 6, 1972, Allen Ginsberg took the Three Refuges of Buddhism. At a ceremony in the Dharmadhatu Meditation Center in Boulder, Colorado, Ginsberg—disaffected Jew, Beat poet, counter culture eminence, gay spokesman, teacher, itinerant bard, political dissident, prankster—pledged to take refuge in the Buddha, the *dharma* (Buddhist teachings) and the *sangha* (the Buddhist community). In addition he took the Bodhisattva vows

---

1. Interview with Henry Tischler, 'Allen Ginsberg—Journals Mid-Fifties: 1954–1958', http://www.authorsspeak.com/ginsberg [all subsequent Website references are http://www].
2. S. Sontag, 'The Aesthetics of Silence' in *A Susan Sontag Reader*, ed. E. Hardwick (Harmondsworth: Penguin, 1983), p181.

which committed him, in the face of inexhaustible obstacles, to work ceaselessly for the liberation of all sentient beings. As part of the ceremony Ginsberg accepted his refuge name of 'Dharma Lion', bestowed by his Tibetan guru, Chögyam Trungpa Rinpoche.[1] This consummated an interest in Buddhism going back to the early 50s. Until his death in April 1997 Ginsberg remained committed to the Buddhist path, and devoted a good deal of his exuberant energies to *dharma* work. For most of the rest of his life he sat in meditation for at least an hour a day and did many extended retreats in which he underwent advanced training in various Buddhist disciplines. He worked enthusiastically on behalf of several Buddhist organizations, particularly the Naropa Institute in Boulder and, in his later years, the Jewel Heart Center in Ann Arbor, Michigan.

Ginsberg's death occasioned much comment on his role in American letters and in the cultural disturbances of the last four decades but, outside the organs of the American Buddhist community, surprisingly little notice was directed to Ginsberg's engagement with Eastern forms of spirituality. Ginsberg's public career and private life (a somewhat slippery distinction in this case!) have been documented in exhausting detail by two recent biographers.[2] There is no point in rehearsing that story here; rather, I want to reflect on his encounter with Asian religious forms. Ginsberg's life and work might be seen as an exemplary site on which various convergences and syntheses take place. Most notably perhaps, we can discern a creative fusion of various polarities and categorizations—East and West, the sacred and profane, the religious and the political, the intellectual and the sensual, the spiritual and the aesthetic.

1. See B. Miles, *Ginsberg: A Biography* (New York: Harper Perennial, 1989), p446.

2. As well as the Miles biography there is Michael Schumacher's *Dharma Lion: A Critical Biography of Allen Ginsberg* (New York: St. Martin's Press, 1992). For a detailed list of critical and biographical work on Ginsberg see 'Writings about Allen Ginsberg',www.charm.net/ffibrooklyn/Biblio/GinsbergBiblio. html.

Ginsberg's Spiritual Trajectory

In retracing his own spiritual growth Ginsberg invariably referred to a pivotal experience in the summer of 1948. At the time he was an undergraduate at Columbia, studying under Lionel Trilling and Mark van Doren, and living in East Harlem. He had already met both William Burroughs and Jack Kerouac with whom he spent a good deal of time discussing 'new consciousness', smoking dope, and experimenting with literary forms which might best capture 'the texture of consciousness' (one of Ginsberg's favorite phrases). He had also embarked on a wide-ranging exploration of the mystical literature of the West, particularly Plotinus, St John of the Cross, St Teresa of Avila, Marvell, and Blake. Here is one of Ginsberg's many accounts of the experience:

> on the sixth floor of a Harlem tenement on 121st Street looking out at the roofs while reading Blake, back and forth, [I] suddenly had an auditory hallucination, hearing Blake—what I thought was his voice, very deep, earthen tone, not very far from my own mature tone of voice... reciting a poem called 'The Sunflower', which I thought expressed some kind of universal longing for union with some infinite nature.... I looked out the window and began to notice the extraordinary detail of the intelligent labor that had gone into the making of the rooftop cornices.... And I suddenly realized that the world was, in a sense, not dead matter, but an increment or deposit of living intelligence and action and activity that finally took form.... And as I looked at the sky I wondered what kind of intelligence had made that vastness, or what was the nature of the intelligence that I was glimpsing, and felt a sense of vastness and of coming home to a space I hadn't realized was there before but which seemed old and infinite, like the Ancient of Days, so to speak.[1]

---

1. A. Ginsberg, 'The Vomit of a Mad Tyger', *Shambhala Sun*, July 1995, shambhalasun.com/ginsberg.html (hereafter 'Tyger').

In a much earlier account Ginsberg described the voice in these terms: 'The peculiar quality of the voice was something unforgettable because it was like God had a human voice, with all the infinite tenderness and mortal gravity of a living Creator speaking to his son.'[1] Elsewhere he called the experience a 'beatific illumination' in which he 'saw the universe unfold in my brain.'[2]

Several other intense experiences, each linked to one of Blake's poems, ensued in the following weeks. All the while Ginsberg was experimenting with drugs—marijuana, peyote, mescaline, later LSD—though no drug-induced experience left as deep an imprint as the 'sunflower episode'. In his researches into Zen Buddhism in the early 50s Ginsberg was struck by the apparent affinities between his own experience and *satori* as described by D.T. Suzuki and others. In fact, Ginsberg remained preoccupied with recreating this experience for the next fifteen years, only snapping out of what he described as a kind of stupe-faction during a meeting in India with Dudjom Rinpoche, head of the Nyingma branch of Tibetan Buddhism. The Rinpoche's adjuration to forego clinging to experiences, whether pleasant or unpleasant, struck home.[3]

In the early 50s Kerouac introduced Ginsberg to several Bud-dhist texts, singing passages from Sanskrit sutras *à la* Frank Sinatra circa 1952.[4] Ginsberg's initial reactions to the rudimen-tary teachings of the Buddha are interesting:

> as an ex-Communist Jewish intellectual, I thought his pronouncement of the First Noble Truth, that existence was suffering, was some sort of insult to my left-wing

---

1. B. Miles, *Ginsberg*, p99. The most detailed account of this experience is found in Ginsberg's interview with Tom Clark in *Paris Review*, Spring, 1966, p37.

2. Ginsberg, quoted in T. Roszak, *The Making of a Counter Culture* (London: Faber, 1969), p127.

3. B. Miles, *Ginsberg*, p104.

4. Allen Ginsberg, excerpt from *Disembodied Poetics: Annals of the Jack Kerouac School*, naropa.edu/ginsbuddhist2.html. Kerouac himself had first turned to these texts in reaction against Neal Cassady's preoccupation with Edgar Cayce—whom Ginsberg later described as a 'crackpot'.

background, since I was a progressive looking forward to the universal improvement of matters....[1]

Ginsberg tells us that it took him two years to accept Kerouac's insistence that the First Noble Truth was 'a very simple fact'. Also crucial to Ginsberg's initiation into the world of Eastern spirituality was his discovery of Chinese painting in the Fine Arts Room of the New York Public Library, an interest in Tibetan iconography (particularly the horrific 'deities') and the *Book of the Dead*. This triggered a lot of 'new mind and eyeball kicks' and inaugurated a massive reading program which included D.T. Suzuki's seminal *Introduction to Zen Buddhism* (1934).[2]

By 1962 Ginsberg—now probably the best-known and certainly the most controversial poet in America—felt the need for a spiritual teacher sufficiently acutely to go on an extended visit to India with his friend and fellow-poet Gary Snyder. Although he visited many holy sites and met a range of distinguished spiritual leaders and teachers (including Swami Shivananda, Dudjom Rinpoche, Gyalwa Karmapa, and the Dalai Lama) Ginsberg did not attach himself to any particular guru nor commit himself to any specific spiritual method.[3] An eclectic mixture of the Hindu and the Buddhist, haphazard meditation of one kind and another, mantra chanting and more drugs remained the order of the day. It was not until 1970 that Swami Muktananda introduced Ginsberg to a systematic meditation practice. However, it was to be Chögyam Trungpa, met briefly in India in 1962, who was to become Ginsberg's guru.

Trungpa was a highly charismatic and controversial figure in American Buddhism. Born in Tibet in 1939, he was identified as a *tulku* (reincarnation of an enlightened teacher) at thirteen months and underwent the intensive Tibetan training culminating in full ordination in the Kagyu sect at the age of eighteen.

---

1. 'Tyger'.

2. B. Miles, *Ginsberg*, p153.

3. For Ginsberg's account of his experiences in India see *Indian Journals, March 1962-May 1963* (San Francisco: City Lights Books & Dave Haselwood Books, 1970). See also B. Miles, *Ginsberg*, chap. 11.

After a highly dramatic escape from Tibet following the Chinese invasion, and a period in India, Trungpa had gone to Oxford to study philosophy, comparative religion and fine art before setting up the Samye-Ling Meditation Centre in Scotland. Some years later he moved to America and was the prime mover in establishing the Naropa Institute in Boulder, Colorado.[1] He was to have a profound impact on Ginsberg—so much so that Ginsberg was later to say that, 'he left such an imprint on my consciousness that I in a sense see through his eyes or see through the same eyes of those occasions where he pointed direction to me.'[2]

After an apparently chance encounter in a New York street in 1970, Trungpa and Ginsberg developed a close and complex relationship—guru and *chela*, philosophical sparring partners, drinking buddies, fellow poets, tricksters, kindred spirits. Under the Tibetan's invitation Ginsberg, with Anne Waldman, set up the Jack Kerouac School of Disembodied Poetics within the Naropa Institute. For many years Ginsberg taught a summer school there which explored the connections between meditation and poetry: 'the life of meditation and the life of art,' he claimed, 'are both based on a similar conception of spontaneous mind. They both share renunciation as a way of avoiding a conditioned art work, or trite art, or repetition of other people's ideas.'[3] Under Trungpa's guidance, he also developed his own meditational practice and deepened his understanding of the Vajrayana tradition in particular (though he retained an interest in Zen Buddhism and Hinduism, as well as later turning back to the Judaism which was his patrimony). It was Trungpa who persuaded Ginsberg to perform improvisational poetry.

1. For a detailed narrative of Trungpa's part in the spread of Buddhism in America see R. Fields, *How the Swans Came to the Lake: A Narrative History of Buddhism in America* (Boston: Shambhala, 1992 rev. edition). For Trungpa's own story of his early life see *Born in Tibet* (Shambhala: Boston, 1995).

2. Canadian Broadcasting Corporation, 'Interview with Allen Ginsberg', myna.com/ffidavidck/giinsbffi1.htm.

3. A. Ginsberg, 'Meditation and Poetics' in *Spiritual Quests: The Art and Craft of Religious Writing*, ed. W. Zinsser (Boston: Houghton Mifflin, 1988), p163.

From the early 70s onwards Ginsberg could properly be described as a serious Buddhist practitioner: as one observer noted in 1976, 'classical Buddhist practice has become the core of Ginsberg's life.'[1] Three years after Trungpa's death in 1986 Philip Glass introduced Ginsberg to another Tibetan master with whom he also developed a close relationship, Kyabje Gelek Rinpoche of the Gelugpa sect, based at the Jewel Heart Center in Ann Arbor, Michigan. Ginsberg himself has noted how the intense devotion and desire which he had previously directed to his literary heroes, friends and multifarious lovers—often to no very good effect—was now largely transferred to the *dharma* and the guru.[2]

Some of the attractions of Buddhism for one of Ginsberg's temperament and experience are plain enough. Buddhism offered a spiritual therapy which could address his deep psychic wounds. Buddhist teachings and meditational practice certainly helped Ginsberg to at least partially heal some of the deep-seated confusions and anxieties, 'elements of resentment, aggression and dead-end anger' which were the legacy of a painful and traumatic childhood. He never lost his sharp sense of life's absurdities but increasingly understood the pain and pathos of the condition to which the Buddha's First Noble Truth alerts us. The form of Buddhism espoused by Trungpa was pragmatic and experiential in method, doctrinally 'open', and free of any disabling associations with either conservative politics or puritanical moralism. Buddhism's non-theistic metaphysic appealed to Ginsberg's anti-authoritarian personality ('there is no Central Intelligence Agency in the universe') and provided a vocabulary in which he could better understand the hierophanies of his student days.[3]

By way of an aside we might note that Ginsberg's various involvements with Tibetan Buddhist organizations in the 70s

1. P.B. Chowka, 'This is Allen Ginsberg?', the 1976 *New Age* Interview, members.aol.com/pbchowka/ginsberg76.html.

2. 'Allen Ginsberg: Anxious Dreams of Eliot', *The Boston Book Review* Interview with Harvey Blume, 1995, www.bookwire.com/bbr/interviews/v2.7/ginsberg.html

3. See 'Tyger'.

and 80s, and the controversies and tensions in which he often found himself involved—most notably the 'Naropa Poetry Wars'[1]—illuminate several aspects of the 'Americanizing' of the Vajrayana. Jack Kornfield has identified democratization (the disassembling of patriarchal and authoritarian power structures, and the move from a monastic to a lay orientation), feminization (the inclusion of women at all levels of practice and leadership), and integration (the adaptation of Buddhist practice to the exigencies of everyday lay life in late 20th century America) as the three key changes in this process.[2] Another conspicuous motif in the development of American Buddhism is the rapid emergence of what has come to be called 'engaged Buddhism'—one dynamically and directly concerned with the most pressing socio-political issues of the day.[3]

Of the many ceremonies that marked Allen Ginsberg's death the Jewel Heart Memorial Service at Ann Arbor was especially poignant. The religious service included both Tibetan and Jewish chants and prayers, and was followed by a concert of poetry and music, read or sung by Ann Waldman, Bob Rosenthal (Ginsberg's personal secretary), Natalie Merchant, and Patti Smith, and including works by Ginsberg, Kerouac, and Bob Dylan. The San Francisco ceremony at the Temple Emmanuel included tributes from Snyder, Diane Di Prima, Lawrence Ferlinghetti, Robert Hass, Joanne Kryger, and Andrew Schelling.[4]

Politics, Poetics and the Western Encounter with Eastern Spirituality

Several questions arise. As the old song has it, 'What's it all about Alfie?' How did this encounter with Buddhism impact on

1. See B. Miles, *Ginsberg*, pp 466–482.

2. See J. Kornfield, 'Is Buddhism Changing in North America?' in *Buddhist America*, ed. Don Morreale (Sante Fe: John Muir Publications, 1988).

3. See F. Eppsteiner (ed.), *The Path of Compassion: Writings on Socially Engaged Buddhism* (Berkeley: Parallax Press, 1988).

4. For information about tributes, ceremonies, remembrances and the like, see: tricycle.com/ginsberg.html

Ginsberg's politics, his aesthetics and his worldview generally? In the context of American cultural transformations what might Ginsberg's experience exemplify? What might we learn from this engagement about the nature of the American experience of Tibetan Buddhism in the second half of the 20th century? What kind of 'divides' did Ginsberg traverse and wherein lies the significance of his spiritual migrations? I do not wish to essay answers to these questions in any very systematic or exhaustive way but rather to offer a few observations which touch on them at various points.

Ginsberg's *persona* and his place in the collective American psyche probably has as much to do with his role as a political gadfly as poet—and indeed he would not have separated the two. From the early Columbia days right down to his death Ginsberg was a burr under the saddle of conservative America, constantly mocking bourgeois values and scandalizing the burghers, puncturing uncomfortable hypocrisies and exposing corruption in the body politic. With his own inimitable mixture of insouciance, *outré* charm, moral gravity and impassioned eloquence he championed causes such as the protection of free expression, gay rights, the ending of the Vietnam War, ecological awareness, the unmasking of American imperialism. All of this is quite unexceptional. What *is* interesting in this context is the way in which Ginsberg's career fuses spiritual and political values, and creates a style and vocabulary of political critique which owes much more to the prophets of ancient Israel, Blake, and Thoreau than to, say, Marx, Bakunin, Goldman—or indeed to Mill, the Webbs, or G.B. Shaw. He had little time for the confrontationist and angry slogans of the SDS and the Weathermen and believed that the rather facile politicization of youth much in evidence in the 60s had somewhat undermined the Beat impulses towards spiritual liberation.[1]

1. See Seth Goddard, 'The Beats and Boom: A Conversation with Allen Ginsberg', pathfinder.com/@@kPiSQwQAOXm@6@3B/Life/boomers/ginberg.html.

Interviewer: Kenneth Rexroth deemed you 'a poet of revolt'... are you still?

Ginsberg: I never have been a poet of revolt, Never never never. That's saying you want to become wiser by becoming dumber, you want to become more peaceful by getting angry.... *My interest is in alteration in consciousness, in new vision*...[this] goes back to 1945 conversations with Kerouac. Revolt of consciousness, ok.[1]

Interviewer: How have you been active in fighting for gay rights?

Ginsberg: I don't believe in fighting.[2]

European radicalism since the 18th century has been, in the main, fiercely secular and militantly atheistic. Institutional religion has been seen, more often than not, as an oppressive and reactionary force and notions of the 'spiritual' and 'mystical' have been variously stigmatized as superstition, obscurantism, alienation, cowardice and neurosis. It is no surprise that Ginsberg should align himself, emotionally and intellectually, with the one significant group of political radicals who did *not* accept the materialistic, positivistic and progressivist assumptions of the Enlightenment, namely the Romantic poets. Nor is it an accident that Romantic values should have figured so largely, though often in caricature, in the counter culture of the 60s. What the counter culture offered was, in Theodore Roszak's word's, 'a defection from the long-standing tradition of skeptical, secular intellectuality which has served as the prime vehicle for three hundred years of scientific and technical work in the West.'[3] Ginsberg's principal role as counter-cultural figure was as a 'vagabond proselytizer' of a this-wordly mysticism, 'an ecstasy of the body and the earth that somehow embraces and

1. 'Allen Ginsberg interviewed by Jeffrey Goldsmith' (italics mine).
2. 'Allen Ginsberg interviewed by Jeffrey Goldsmith'.
3. T. Roszak, *The Making of a Counter Culture*, p141.

transforms mortality . . . a joy that includes . . . the commonplace obscenities of our existence.'[1]

Ginsberg's 'beatific illuminations' and his subsequent immersion in Indian, Tibetan and Japanese spirituality gave him a perspective and a metaphysic which certainly did not blunt his political radicalism but which provided a certain distance, a sense of proportion, and a scale of values which moved him past an adolescent rage at the cultural wasteland of Ike and Dale Carnegie and Lassie, and the 'single vision' of a materialistic gospel of progress, and beyond the narrow, antagonistic dichotomies of Marxist rhetoric and the easy sentimentalities of Utopianism in its manifold guises. Increasingly his political stance, and indeed his poetry, seemed to derive less from the impulse to mockery, from hatred and alienation, and more from a sense of compassion—remember that in the Buddhist context compassion (*karuna*) is inseparable from wisdom (*prajna*) of which it is actually the dynamic aspect. Ginsberg's later interviews often evince the non-combative and compassionate values which lie at the heart of the Buddhist tradition.

In a larger context we might ponder the significance of the changes whereby the iconic figures of the secular left (say, Lenin, Emma Goldman, Trotsky, Joe Hill) have lost a good deal of their luster whilst those whose radicalism is governed by a 'politics of eternity' (say, Gandhi, Thich Nhat Hanh, the Dalai Lama) take on a new aura. This answers to something much deeper than the whimsies of political fashion. It is tempting to believe that a new paradigm of socio-political transformation is still being fashioned—one drawing on the European post-Enlightenment, radical mainstream but discarding its one-dimensional materialism and utilitarian rationality (and the scientistic ideologies from which they derive), and much more receptive to the spiritual messages of both our own largely-forgotten tradition and of non-Western cultures alike.

Mark Linenthal has claimed, persuasively enough, that Ginsberg, 'more than any other writer changed what a whole

1. Ibid., p129.

generation thought a poem should or could be.'[1] Our interest here is not so much in the literary upheaval unleashed by the first public reading of 'Howl' (1955)—the 'most widely sold, read, and discussed poem of the decade'[2]—but rather in the inter-relationships of aesthetics, politics and metaphysics in Ginsberg's life/work. Clearly the 'alteration in consciousness' of which he so often spoke encompasses all of these dimensions. Ginsberg once defined classical poetry as 'a 'process', or experiment—a probe into the nature of reality and the nature of the mind.'[3] How easily the definition fits Buddhism itself. Ginsberg repeatedly talks of 'new consciousness' as providing the emergent Beat writers with their focal point and as impelling their interest in writers such as Blake, Rimbaud, Baudelaire, and Yeats ('our great grandfathers among hermetic poets and philosophers').[4] Of course, since time immemorial poetry has been the medium in which the religious sensibility most readily and fully expresses itself—think of Homer, the Psalms, the rhapsodies of the Vedic rishis.[5] 'Poet is Priest', as Ginsberg puts it in the first line of 'Death to Van Gogh's Ear'.

The Beats' search for new consciousness and for new poetic forms, their rejection of the General Motors/Walt Disney version of the American Dream, their impulse to escape the grip of Urizen (Blake's mythical personification of 'Single Vision'—instrumentalist rationality, the Human Imagination petrified, Newton's Pantocrator) were all of a piece:

> We didn't have what you would call a philosophy. I would say there was an ethos, that there were ideas... themes... preoccupations... *the primary thing was a move towards spiritual*

---

1. 'San Francisco Says Goodbye to a Bard', *San Francisco Chronicle*, April 21, 1997, a1.

2. D. Hoffman (ed), *Harvard Guide to Contemporary American Writing* (Cambridge: The Belknap Press, 1979), p519.

3. A. Ginsberg, 'Meditation and Poetics', p145.

4. Ibid., p148.

5. On this subject see B. Griffiths, *The Marriage of East and West* (London: Collins, 1982), pp47ff.

liberation, not merely from Bourgeois, 50s quietism, or Silent Generation, but from the last centuries of mechanization and homogenization of cultures, the mechanical assault on human nature and all nature culminating in the bomb . . . the search for new consciousness. . . . I don't think we had it clearly defined, but we were looking for something . . . as a kind of breakthrough from the sort of hyper-rationalistic, hyper-scientific, hyper-rationalizing of the post-war era.[1]

As Michael McClure put it in his memoir *Scratching the Beat Surface*, 'None of us wanted to go back to the gray, chill, militaristic silence, to the intellective void—to the land without poetry—to the spiritual drabness. We wanted to make it new. . . . We wanted voice and we wanted vision.'[2] Here indeed were 'angelheaded hipsters burning for ancient heavenly connection'! In this context it is no surprise that a good many of the Beat circle developed a serious and sustained interest in aspects of Eastern religion, art and philosophy—Kerouac, Snyder, Kenneth Rexroth, Philip Whalen, Anne Waldman amongst them.

The whole literary experiment of the Beats, at least for Ginsberg (and certainly for Kerouac and Snyder) was impelled by a spiritual rather than an aesthetic aspiration. Or, to put it differently, the new literary forms emerged out of the explorations of consciousness rather than out of any coherent aesthetic theory, and certainly not out of any blind iconoclasm. As is so often the case with *avant-garde* movements in whatever domain, theory *followed* practice. As Ginsberg himself succinctly characterized the Beat movement: 'a spiritual revolution that took form in the changes in the literary method. . . .'[3] Or again, to put the point

1. S. Goddard, 'The Beats and Boom: A Conversation with Allen Ginsberg' (italics mine). See also 'Allen Ginsberg interviewed by Jeffrey Goldsmith' where Ginsberg says, 'My own idea is that the origins of beat writings were in some kind of spiritual revolution.'

2. S. Silberman, 'How Beat Happened', ezone.org:1080/ez/e2/articles/digaman.html

3. S. Goddard, 'The Beats and Boom: A Conversation with Allen Ginsberg'.

differently, poetry, for Ginsberg, became a form of spiritual practice—and one nicely attuned to the spiritual economy of Buddhism with its pervasive concern with 'the texture of consciousness', underpinned by a metaphysic of 'emptiness' or 'voidness' (*sunyata*) which, far from constituting a nihilistic negation, provided the basis for what Ginsberg called 'continuous generous activity, exuberant activity,' without hope or fear, non-attached, and compassionate—in short, *karuna*.[1] Ginsberg repeatedly foregrounds the intersections of meditational practice and the writing of poetry: in each case it is a matter of

> noticing my thoughts, noticing that I'm noticing it, observing what's there, then realizing what is really there... being a stenographer of your own mind... scanning your mind and observing your thoughts, and what forms arise and flourish.[2] [Thus] there's a natural affinity between non-theistic practice and up to date modern and post-modern American poetic practice.[3]

Ginsberg, like other artists and intellectuals who have turned Eastwards, also had a role to play in what Mircea Eliade has called the 'deprovincializing' of Western culture in a 'crepuscular era'.[4] The epoch of self-contained and more or less homogeneous civilizations is, of course, long since gone. As Lyotard remarked of the 'postmodernist' condition, 'One listens to reggae, watches a western, eats McDonald's food for lunch and local cuisine for dinner, wears Paris perfume in Tokyo and "retro" clothes in Hong Kong.'[5] He might have added something about mantras, mandalas, mudras, or maharishis! The cultural

1. Ibid.
2. J. Moore, 'Public Heart: An Interview with Allen Ginsberg', bookwire. com/hmr/REVIEW/moore.html.
3. Canadian Broadcasting Corporation, 'Interview with Allen Ginsberg'.
4. See M. Eliade, *Autobiography II: 1937–1960, Exile's Odyssey* (Chicago: University of Chicago, 1988), pp152–153, and *The Quest: History and Meaning in Religion* (Chicago: University of Chicago, 1969), pp62–63.
5. Jean-François Lyotard quoted in T. Gitlin, 'Style for style's sake' in *The Weekend Australian*, January 21–22, 1989, Weekender, p9.

fabric itself becomes a Barthesian text, 'a tissue of quotations drawn from the innumerable centres of culture.'[1] In Ginsberg's case it was a matter of a disaffiliated American Jew of Russian background careering around America chanting Hindu mantras, reciting Blake and Whitman, playing an Indian harmonium and Aboriginal song sticks, expounding Tibetan metaphysics, quoting Milarepa, Jewish mystics, and the Sixth Patriarch.

On one level one might suppose that a good deal of the Beat/counter-cultural infatuation with the exotic, the 'oriental', the 'mystical' and 'magical' was indeed of a sentimental and fashionable order. Doubtless, there was a good deal of counterfeit spirituality peddled by false gurus, by charlatans and hucksters, as there is today under the canopy of New Age-ism. But, no question, the interest in Eastern spirituality met some deep yearning for *a vision of reality* deeper, richer, more adequate, more attuned to the fullness of human experience, than the impoverished worldview offered by a scientifically-grounded humanism. In short, the Beats and the hippies said 'no way José!' to the 'grand narrative' of the Enlightenment, and turned to other sources for the wellsprings of wisdom and individual/collective well-being—the religious traditions of the East, the beliefs and practices of indigenous cultures, the quasi-mystical experiences apparently offered by drugs, the mythology and mystical literature enshrined in the pre-Renaissance traditions of the West, and the like.

A serious American engagement with Eastern religions goes back at least to Emerson and Thoreau: the Beats counted the Transcendentalists amongst their progenitors.[2] Other obvious precursors include the Theosophists of the late 19th century and the Vedantists of the inter-war period (the latter originating in the World Parliament of Religions in Chicago in 1893). The Beat and counter-cultural involvement in Eastern spirituality was not

---

1. R. Barthes, 'The Death of the Author' in *Image Music Text*, ed. Stephen Heath (London: Fontana, 1977), p146.
2. See R. Fields, *How the Swans Came to the Lake: A Narrative History of Buddhism in America*, chap. 4.

without precedent; nor was it either ephemeral or trivial and, indeed, it is still bearing fruit. The adherence of a rapidly growing and highly significant portion of the Western intelligentsia— artists, writers, philosophers, social activists prominently—to Eastern religious forms (most notably from the Tibetan and Japanese branches of Buddhism), and the assimilation of Asian modes of spiritual experience and cultural expression into Western forms, is one of the more remarkable cultural metamorphoses of the late 20th century, one as yet barely recognized let alone understood. More particularly, the impact of the Tibetan diaspora on the West, especially the USA, demands more serious attention.

Swami Abhishiktananda, Fr Jules Monchanin *and the* Hindu-Christian Encounter

Let the athlete of the spirit ever integrate himself
Standing in a place apart,
alone, his thoughts and self restrained,
Devoid of earthly hope, possessing nothing.
(Bhagavad Gita vi.10)

Background: Christian Missionizing in the East

It is no secret that over the last century Christian missionizing in India has had a bad press. The Theosophists, neo-Hindu reformers, Western Vedantins, fictionalists such as Somerset Maugham, historians, and the post-colonial critics, have all lambasted the whole missionary enterprise. The auxiliary role of Christian missionizing in the spread of European imperialism and in the extirpation of traditional cultures has, quite properly, come under attack. However, it must also be recognized that the enemies of Christianity (and often of religion in general) are ever-ready to portray its representatives in the worst possible light, to attribute to them the most sinister of motives and to attribute to them all manner of ills. Certainly there is no hiding from the dismal fact that an arrogant and intolerant Christian exclusivism has sometimes been an accomplice in rapacious empire-building. At the same time, it is as well to remember that missionaries often resisted and condemned the exploitative aspects of imperialism. Recent scholarship has confirmed 'the great variety of missionary relationships to and attitudes toward imperialism, so that no generalization, save that of variety, can be maintained'.[1] Furthermore, we need to recognize the creative role missionaries have played in nurturing a deeper understanding of the religious heritage of the East. Recall the pioneering work of the Jesuits in India, Tibet, China and Japan in dispelling European ignorance about Asian religions: the legacy of men such as Fathers Nobili, Desideri, Matteo Ricci, and Francis Xavier in promoting a dialogue between West and East and in opening European eyes to the spiritual riches of the East cannot be easily ignored. Think, too, of the role of missionaries who have, in some sense, become advocates of Asian religious and philosophical traditions *against* the European values and assumptions which they themselves ostensibly represent: one thinks of figures such as Dwight Goddard, Richard Wilhelm, and, more recently, the comparative religionist Klaus Klostermaier and the missionary-sinologist, D.H. Smith. In recent times missionaries have often been in the vanguard of movements for national liberation and the achievement of human rights and social justice. So, the story of missionary activity is a complex one. In this article another aspect of this complex phenomenon is explored: the way in which a missionizing enterprise is sometimes transformed into a profound inter-religious encounter. The focus will be on two Benedictine monks, Fathers Jules Monchanin and Henri Le Saux, whose contrasting experiences in India illuminate a whole series of issues inherent in inter-religious encounters generally and, more specifically, in the ongoing intercourse between Christianity and Hinduism.

---

1. C.W. Forman, 'The growth of the study of the expansion of Christianity', *Religious Studies Review* 13.1, 1987, p32. See also S. Lund, 'The Christian Mission and Colonialism', *Temenos* 17, 1981, pp116–123.

Christian Missionaries
and the Christian-Hindu Encounter

Vasco da Gama arrived in the south Indian port of Calicut in 1498, and Pedro Cabral in Cochin two years later. The search for spices was soon joined by the quest for souls. The earliest European missionaries in India were Franciscans and Dominicans, soon to be followed by the redoubtable Jesuits. By the middle of the 16th century the Jesuits were entrenched in Goa and its hinterland, and well-advanced on their first major task—the mastery of the principal languages of the region. In 1579 the British Jesuit Thomas Stephens arrived in Goa and was soon able to produce several works in Indian languages, culminating in his 11,000-verse *Christian Purana*, 'the unsurpassed masterpiece of Christian missionary literature in an Indian vernacular.' But it was Father Roberto Nobili (1577–1656) who 'led the missionary effort to an entirely new level of theoretical and hermeneutic awareness' and who best exemplifies 'the problematic nature of the encounter between Christianity and Hinduism'.[1] His efforts to find some sort of doctrinal rapprochement between the two traditions inevitably overstepped ecclesiastical bounds. Nobili found in the *Upanishads* a pristine monotheism and even intimations of the 'recondite mystery of the most sacred trinity', discerned the 'natural light' of reason in Brahminical sciences and philosophy, and argued against their dismissal by Europeans as superstitious, 'as if the heathen sages were not also bringing forth valuable teachings which could likewise be of use to Christians.'[2] Nobili found some precedent for his approach to Hinduism in the reception of Greek thought by the early Fathers. Nobili in turn served as an inspiration for Father Bede Griffiths (1906–1993), an English Benedictine monk in India three centuries later. Nor was Nobili playing a lone hand. Heinrich Roth (1620–1668) produced the first European Sanskrit grammar,

---

1. W. Halbfass, *India and Europe: An Essay in Philosophical Understanding* (Delhi: Motilal Banarsidass, 1990), pp37–38.
    2. Ibid., p40.

philosophical commentaries and translations. Father J.F. Pons, another Jesuit, was probably the author of a grammar of Sanskrit in Latin in about 1733. Then, too, there were the Protestant missionary scholars such as the Dutch Calvinists Abraham Roger and Philippus Baldaeus who published Indological works in the 17th century, and the Moravian Bartholomäus Ziegenbalg who wrote substantial hermeneutical works on the customs and beliefs of the Hindus.

In his remarkable study of the encounter between India and Europe, Wilhelm Halbfass points out that the work of the missionaries of the seventeenth and eighteenth centuries laid the foundations of Indological research well before the appearance of the Asiatic Society of Bengal in 1784 and the pioneering scholarship of Jones, Wilkins and Colebrooke, the first British Orientalists-proper. The legacy of the Jesuits was to be found not only in their texts—grammars, dictionaries, translations, commentaries and the like—but in the collection of manuscripts and their development of methods of collaboration with Indian scholars.[1]

By the mid-19th century the missionary ethos was increasingly influenced by the idea of 'fulfilment', foreshadowed in some of Nobili's writings and embryonic in the ideas of Max Müller and Monier-Williams. The missionary and Indologist J.N. Farquhar was perhaps its most influential exponent. Thus, following T.E. Slater's claim that 'All religions wait for their fulfilment in Christianity,' Farquhar could argue that

> The Vedanta is not Christianity, and never will be—simply as the Vedanta: but a very definite preparation for it.... It is our belief that the living Christ will sanctify and make complete the religious thought of India. For centuries... her saints have been longing for him, and her thinkers, not least the thinkers of the Vedanta have been thinking his thought.[2]

1. Ibid., p45.
2. Farquhar quoted in W. Halbfass, ibid., p51.

Furthermore,

> This is the attitude of Jesus to all other religions also. Each contains a partial revelation of God's will, but each is incomplete; and He comes to fulfil them all. In each case Christianity seeks not to destroy but to take all that is right and raise it to perfection.[1]

This idea was later to find an ironic echo in the neo-Hindu claim that all other religions and creeds are subsumed by Vedanta. (One might adduce Swami Vivekananda as one amongst many spokesmen for this claim.)

During the 20th century many missionary societies and individual missionaries have had to come to terms with the palpable historical fact that, in India at least (and indeed most other Asian countries, the Philippines and to a lesser extent Korea, being the notable exceptions), Christian triumphalism was quite misplaced, that the rates of conversion are pitifully small, that while most Hindus are perfectly willing to accept Christ as one *avatar* among many, they remain impervious to the fulfilment theory and its many variants. So much for the kind of thinking behind Macaulay's boast in 1836 that English education would see to it that thirty years hence 'there will not be a single idolator [i.e., Hindu] among the respectable classes in Bengal.'[2] The general failure of Christian missionaries to win significant number of converts eventually moved the accent of mission work onto ideals of witness, service and dialogue rather than conversion. However, it would be a mistake to measure the validity of the missionary enterprise purely in terms of conversion rates. As Frithjof Schuon has remarked,

> [Christian] missionaries—although they have profited from abnormal circumstances inasmuch as Western expansion at the expense of other civilizations is due solely to a crushing

---

1. Farquhar quoted in E. Sharpe, *Not to Destroy but to Fulfil* (Upsalla: Gleerup, 1965), p260.
2. T.B. Macaulay, *Letters of Lord Macaulay* (London: Longman, 1876), p455.

material superiority arising out of the modern deviation—follow a way that possesses, at least in principle, a sacrificial aspect; consequently the subjective reality of this way will always retain its mystic meaning.[1]

Surveying over three centuries of European missionizing in India, Wilhelm Halbfass concludes that

> the missionary efforts in this country can hardly be described as having been successful, and dogmatism and intolerance have frequently played a dominating role.... This notwithstanding, the achievements of the missionaries comprise a very important chapter in the Western encounter with Indian thought, a chapter that is exemplary from a hermeneutic standpoint and which, moreover, has had historical consequences. The missionaries have performed pioneering, detailed work in several areas. But primarily, in spite of or perhaps precisely because of their 'prejudice' and dogmatic limitations, they have also helped to define and clarify the central problems involved in approaching and understanding that which is alien...their outstanding exponents embody a desire to understand whose singular power and problematic nature arise from their deep and uncompromising desire to be understood.[2]

The 'problematic nature' of missionizing is dramatically personified in the 20th century in the lives and work of three Benedictine monks, each of whom wished to reconcile Hinduism and Christianity: Jules Monchanin, Henri Le Saux and Bede Griffiths. Certain themes and issues circulate through the experiences and writings of each: the so-called 'problem' of religious pluralism, the proper role of Christianity in India, the renewal of Christian monasticism and the revival of its contemplative and mystical heritage, the doctrinal reconciliation of Advaita Vedanta with a Trinitarian Christianity, the existential problem

1. F. Schuon, *The Transcendent Unity of Religions* (New York: Harper & Row, 1975, rev. ed.), p81.
2. W. Halbfass, *Indian and Europe*, p53.

of living out a spirituality which drew on both Eastern and Western sources. Because the work of Bede Griffiths is already today pretty well known in the West, we will here focus on Monchanin and Le Saux, situating them in the problematic of the modern encounter of Hinduism and Christianity.

Father Jules Monchanin
(Swami Arubianandam)

The first forty years of Jules Monchanin's life were unexceptional for a provincial French priest.[1] He was born near Lyons in 1895, decided at an early age to enter the priesthood and completed his theological training in 1922. Despite his intellectual distinction he did not complete his doctoral studies but instead asked to be sent to a miners' parish in a poor suburb of Lyons. He served in three parishes before a serious illness was followed by appointments as a chaplain, first in an orphanage and then at a boys' boarding school. Throughout these years he continued to move in a university milieu and applied himself to a range of studies. Since boyhood he had felt an attraction to India which now steered him towards Sanskrit, and Indological and comparative religious studies. From the early 30s Monchanin was exploring the possibility of living some sort of Christian monastic life in India, no easy task for someone bound to Mother Church. It took many years of negotiations before he finally received the approval of the Bishop of Tiruchirapalli to work amongst the scattered Indian Christians in the region evangelized centuries before by both Francis Xavier and Roberto Nobili. Monchanin left Marseilles for India in May 1939.

For the next decade Monchanin was immersed in pastoral work in India. These were years of social deprivation, physical hardship, and acute loneliness, preparatory to the contemplative

---

1. Most of the biographical material following is taken from J.G. Weber, *In Quest of the Absolute: the Life and Work of Jules Monchanin* (Kalamazoo: Cistercian Publications, 1977).

life for which he yearned. At last, in 1950, he was able to establish a monastic hermitage on the banks of the Kavery River, a Christian ashram which he and his fellow Benedictine and compatriot, Henri le Saux, called 'Saccidananda'. ('*Saccidananda*': Brahman, or the Ultimate Reality, conceived of as Being, Sentience and Bliss; sometimes paralleled with the Christian Trinity.) Le Saux articulated their agenda:

> Our goal: to form the first nucleus of a monastery (or rather a laura, a grouping of neighboring anchorites like the ancient laura of Saint Sabas in Palestine) which buttresses the Rule of Saint Benedict—a primitive, sober, discrete rule. Only one purpose: to seek God. And the monastery will be Indian style. We would like to crystallize and transubstantiate the search of the Hindu *sannyasi*. Advaita and the praise of the Trinity are our only aim. This means we must grasp the authentic Hindu search for God in order to Christianize it, starting with ourselves first of all, from within.[1]

Vedantic philosophy, Christian theology, Indian lifestyle. Their hope was that 'what is deepest in Christianity may be grafted on to what is deepest in India.'[2] This was not a syncretic exercise which would issue forth some religious hybrid but an attempt to fathom the depths of Christianity with the aid of the traditional wisdom of India which, in the monks' view, was to be found in Vedanta and the spiritual disciplines of the renunciate. The lifestyle was to be thoroughly Indian: meditation, prayer, study of the Scriptures of both traditions, a simple vegetarian diet, the most Spartan of amenities. Each donned the ochre cloth of the *sannyasin*, Monchanin (informally) becoming Swami Arubianandam and Le Saux Swami Abhishiktananda.

Monchanin had alluded earlier to the case of Dom Joliet, a French naval officer in China who became a Benedictine in 1897

1. J.G. Weber, *In Quest of the Absolute*, p73.
2. Ibid., p2.

and waited thirty years to realize his dream of founding a Christian monastery in the Far East. Monchanin had written, 'Will I someday know the same joy, that in India too—from its soil and spirit—there will come a [Christian] monastic life dedicated to contemplation?'[1] The dream was not to be fully realized in Monchanin's lifetime. On the face of it, the efforts of the French monks were less than successful: it was a constant struggle to keep the ashram afloat; there was little enthusiasm from either European or Indian quarters; there were endless difficulties and hardships; not a solitary Indian monk became a permanent member of the ashram. By the time of Monchanin's death in 1957 there seemed little to show for the hard years behind them. Monchanin was not even able to realize his desire to die in India as he had been sent to Paris for medical treatment. But the seeds had been sown. A decade after Monchanin's death, Father Bede Griffiths and two Indian monks left their own ashram and committed themselves to Saccidananda ashram. There were to be many difficult years still ahead, but Monchanin's dream finally came to fruition under Bede Griffiths who later wrote of Monchanin's mission:

> The ashram which he founded remains as a witness to the ideal of a contemplative life which he had set before him, and his life and writings remain to inspire others with the vision of a Christian contemplation which shall have assimilated the wisdom of India, and a theology in which the genius of India shall find expression in Christian terms.[2]

In Monchanin we find a formidable intellect, considerable erudition, and a refined sensibility with an appreciation of Europe's cultural heritage; he might easily have fashioned a splendid academic or ecclesiastical career. We have the testimony of some of the leading French Indologists of the day to this effect. His closest associate, Le Saux, said of him,

1. Ibid., pp 21–22.
2. Ibid., p 3.

He was one of the most brilliant intellects among the French clergy, a remarkable conversationalist, at home on every subject, a brilliant lecturer and a theologian who opened before his hearers marvellous and ever new horizons.[1]

Instead, all is surrendered to plunge himself into the materially impoverished life of the Indian villager and the eremitic life of the monk, the Christian *sannyasi.* In 1941 he had written in his journal, 'May India take me and bury me within itself—in God.'[2] It was a noble ideal.

The annals of Christian missionizing are replete with stories of heroic self-sacrifice, of dedication to tireless, often thankless work in arid fields, an exacting and lonely life in the service of Christian ideals—precisely, the pursuit of a vocation. Monchanin, however, is a fascinating case because in him the missionary dilemma, if one may so express it, becomes fully and acutely self-conscious. The poignancy and tragedy of Monchanin's life in India is that he was unable to find his way out of the dilemma. Here is a telling passage from the autobiography of Alain Daniélou, the French scholar who lived for many years in India, committed himself to Hinduism, and produced some imposing work on the Indian tradition:

> Then there was the curious little ashram of Père Montchanin (sic). This priest ... had been deeply influenced by Hinduism and wanted to combine the two religions. He wore the draped orange cloth of Hindu monks, but obviously did not perform the ritual ablutions ... he lived in a hermitage with a few followers and exerted a great influence on that special brand of foreigner who, while acknowledging the spiritual, philosophical, and moral superiority of Hinduism, still insists on Christian supremacy.... Instead of mellowing through Hinduism, Montchanin and his devotees remained

1. Abhishiktananda quoted in E. Vattakuzhy, *Indian Christian Sannyasa and Swami Abhishiktananda* (Bangalore: Theological Publications in India, 1981), p67.

2. J.G. Weber, *In Quest of the Absolute,* p56.

frustrated, neurotic, ill at ease, and, on the whole, rather dis-
agreeable people. . . .[1]

This passage itself might be seen by some as somewhat 'dis-
agreeable', lacking in charity, and tainted with that condescen-
sion which is sometimes the mark of the Western 'Vedantin'.
Nonetheless, it is insightful. It is clear from Monchanin's own
writings that he intuitively understood 'the limits of religious
expansionism' (to borrow a phrase from Frithjof Schuon). He
was intelligent enough to see that insofar as Christians were
bent on converting Indians, the enterprise was doomed to failure (the odd individual convert being the exception that proves
the rule). He rightly sensed that devout Hindus found the idea
of conversion abhorrent—'a betrayal, cowardice.'[2] Shortly
before his death he wrote,

> The root of the matter is that Hindus are not spiritually
> uneasy. They believe they possess supreme wisdom and
> thus how could they attach any importance to the fluctua-
> tions or investigations of those who possess lesser wisdom.
> Christ is one among *avataras*. Christianity in their eyes is a
> perfect moral doctrine, but a metaphysics which stops on
> the threshold of the ultimate metamorphosis.[3]

He was also, as Daniélou intimates, well-equipped to appreci-
ate the vast storehouse of Indian spirituality. But throughout his
life he felt bound to the conventional Christian belief in the ultimate superiority of his own faith, a position to which he was
theologically committed by the weight of the centuries. His
friend Père Henri de Lubac had characterized Monchanin's task
this way: 'to rethink everything in the light of theology, and to
rethink theology through mysticism.'[4] The problem was that the

---

1. A. Daniélou, *The Way to the Labyrinth: Memories of East and West* (New York:
New Directions, 1987), p213.

2. J.G. Weber, *In Quest of the Absolute*, p92.

3. Ibid., p97.

4. Ibid., p25.

theology and the mysticism were pulling in opposite directions, the tension arising out of a dogmatic literalism and an ossified exotericism in the Catholic Church which insisted on the *exclusive* truths of Christianity and, *ipso facto*, on its *superiority* to other faiths. During a near-fatal illness in 1932 Monchanin had vowed that, if he were to recover, he would devote himself to the salvation of India: his years in India taught him, at least sub-consciously, that India (insofar as it still cleaved to its own traditions) was in no need of salvation! Consider a few quotes from Monchanin's writings:

India has stood for three millennia, if not longer, as the seat of one of the principal civilizations of mankind, equal to if not greater than that of Europe and China....

India has received from the Almighty an uncommon gift, an unquenchable thirst for whatever is spiritual. Since the time of the *Vedas* and the *Upanishads*, countless numbers of its sons have been great seekers of God.

Century after century there rose up seers and poets singing the joys and sorrows of a soul in quest of the One, and philosophers reminding every man of the supremacy of contemplation....

Cheek by jowl with lofty passages such as these we find quite contradictory ones:

Unfortunately Indian wisdom is tainted with erroneous tendencies.... Outside the unique revelation and the unique Church man is always and everywhere incapable of sifting truth from falsehood and good from evil.

So also, confident in the indefectible guidance of the Church, we hope that India, once baptized into the fullness of its body and soul and into the depth of its age-long quest for Brahma, will reject its pantheistic tendencies and, discovering in the splendors of the Holy Spirit the true

mysticism and finding at last the vainly longed-for philosophical and theological equilibrium between antagonistic
trends of thought, will bring forth for the good of humanity
and the Church and ultimately for the glory of God unpar-
alleled galaxies of saints and doctors.

[We] cannot hide [Hinduism's] fundamental error and its
essential divergence in terms of Christianity. Hinduism
must reject its *atman-brahman* equation, if it is to enter into
Christ.[1]

The tensions between a rigid Christian exclusivism and a
recognition of the spiritual depths of Hinduism could hardly be
more apparent. Monchanin's life would have been much easier
had the Vatican II renovation of Catholic attitudes to other
religions taken place half a century earlier. (Vatican II was, in
common parlance, a 'a very mixed bag' but the mitigation of
centuries of exclusivism was a significant step in the right
direction.) Monchanin might also have been spared much
agonizing by recourse to the works of traditionalists such as his
fellow countryman, René Guénon, or Frithjof Schuon. Seyyed
Hossein Nasr states the problem concisely:

The essential problem that the study of religion poses is
how to preserve religious truth, traditional orthodoxy, the
dogmatic theological structures of one's own tradition, and
yet gain knowledge of other traditions and accept them as
spiritually valid ways and roads to God.[2]

This was the problem which Monchanin could never quite
overcome. His successor, Bede Griffiths, was able at least partially to resolve the dilemma by discerning that the task at hand
was not to 'Christianize' Hinduism—an undertaking to which
the Indians themselves remained, for the most part, supremely
indifferent—but to 'Hinduize' Christianity, that is, to recover

1. Monchanin in J.G. Weber, *In Quest of the Absolute*, pp77–78, 82, 126.
2. S.H. Nasr, *Sufi Essays* (London: Allen & Unwin, 1972), p127.

the mystical and contemplative dimension of the Christian tradition and its metaphysical underpinnings, by recourse to a sapiential wisdom and a more or less intact spiritual methodology still comparatively untouched by the ravages of modernity. This became the governing impulse of Griffiths' life and work in his later years in India and is evident in such works as *Return to the Centre* (1976) and *The Marriage of East and West* (1982).

Henri Le Saux
(Swami Abhishiktananda)

Henri Le Saux arrived in India in 1948 to join Monchanin in the monastic venture at Shantivanam. He was never to leave the shores of his adopted country. Le Saux was born in Brittany in 1910 and entered a Benedictine monastery in 1929. Like Monchanin he felt the call of India as a young man but he too had to endure a lengthy wait before achieving 'his most ardent desire', and embarking for the sub-continent. Soon after setting up the modest ashram the two French Benedictines travelled to Arunachala to visit Ramana Maharshi who made the most profound impression on Le Saux:

> Even before my mind was able to recognize the fact, and still less to express it, the invisible halo of this Sage had been perceived by something in me deeper than any words. Unknown harmonies awoke in my heart.... In the Sage of Arunachala of our time I discerned the Unique Sage of the eternal India, the unbroken succession of her sages, her ascetics, her seers; it was as if the very soul of India penetrated to the very depths of my own soul and held mysterious communion with it. It was a call which pierced through everything, rent it in pieces and opened a mighty abyss....[1]

1. O. Baumer-Despeigne, 'The Spiritual Journey of Henri Le Saux-Swami Abhishiktananda', *Cistercian Studies*, 18, 1983, p313.

It is interesting to compare this with a strikingly similar account of the Maharishi's nature and significance by Schuon:

> In Sri Ramana Maharshi one meets again ancient and eternal India. The Vedantic truth—the truth of the Upanishads —is brought back to its simplest expression but without any kind of betrayal.... Sri Ramana was as it were the incarnation, in these latter days and in the face of modern activist fever, of what is primordial and incorruptible in India. He manifested the nobility of contemplative 'non-action' in the face of an ethic of utilitarian agitation and he showed the implacable beauty of pure truth in the face of passions, weaknesses and betrayals.[1]

In the years following Ramana's death Le Saux spent two extended periods as a hermit in one of the holy mountain's many caves. He wrote of an overwhelming mystical experience while in retreat at Arunachala and stated that he was 'truly reborn at Arunachala under the guidance of the Maharishi,'[2] understanding 'what is beyond silence: *sunyata*.' 'Ramana's *Advaita* is my birthplace. Against that all rationalization is shattered.'[3] He also became a disciple of Sri Gnanananda Giri of Tiruykoyilur, giving an account of this in *Guru and Disciple* (1967) and *The Secret of Arunachala* (1974). He remarks that upon meeting Gnanananda he *automatically* yielded his allegiance to him, something which he had never previously done.[4]

Over the next few years Abhishiktananda gradually loosened his connections with the ashram at Shantivanam and spent much of his time as a wandering *sannyasi* in the Himalayas. It was his impregnable conviction that the life of renunciation was the meeting point of Christianity and Hinduism:

---

1. F. Schuon, *Language of the Self* (Madras: Ganesh, 1959), p44.

2. J.M.D. Stuart, 'Sri Ramana Maharshi and Abhishiktananda', *Vidjajyoti*, April 1980, p170.

3. O. Baumer-Despeigne, 'The Spiritual Journey of Henri Le Saux', p316.

4. J.E. Royster, 'Abhishiktananda: Hindu-Christian Monk', *Studies in Formative Spirituality*, 9:3, 1988, p311.

Believe me, it is above all in the mystery of *sannyasa* that India and the Church will meet, will discover themselves in the most secret and hidden parts of their hearts, in the place where they are each most truly themselves, in the mystery of their origin in which every outward manifestation is rooted and from which time unfolds itself.[1]

He formalized his Indian citizenship in 1960 (he had long been a spiritual citizen), and founded a small hermitage on the banks of the Ganges at Uttarkashi in the Himalayas. Here he plunged ever deeper into the *Upanishads*, realizing more and more the Church's need of India's timeless message. He also consolidated his grasp of Sanskrit, Tamil and English, and often participated in retreats, conferences and inter-faith gatherings. It was appropriate that most of his books were written here, near the source of the Ganges. In his last two years he gathered a small group of disciples, including Marc Chaduc (Swami Ajatananda).[2] Abhishiktananda died in 1973. In his final illness he had experienced again 'an inner apocalypse', 'an awakening beyond all myths and symbols',[3] returning him to one of his favorite Upanishadic verses (of which we can find echoes in many mystical works of both East and West):

> *I know him, that great Purusha*
> *Of the color of the sun,*
> *Beyond all darkness.*
> *He who has known him*
> *Goes beyond death.*
> *There is no other way.*
> (Svetasvatara Upanishad, III.8)

He wrote in one of his last letters, 'the quest is fulfilled.'[4]
Abhishiktananda seems to have had a more natural affinity for

---

1. Abhishiktananda, *Guru and Disciple* (London: SPCK, 1974), p162.
2. See A. Rawlinson, *The Book of Enlightened Masters* (Chicago: Open Court, 1997), pp146–150.
3. O. Baumer-Despeigne, 'The Spiritual Journey of Henri Le Saux', pp327–328.
4. Ibid., p329.

the actual practices of Hindu spirituality than did Monchanin and was less troubled by the doctrinal tensions between the two traditions which he was seeking to bridge. It is surely significant that it was Abhishiktananda who was able to surrender to the extraordinary *darsan* of Ramana. It is also suggestive that, of the three Benedictines associated with Saccidananda Ashram, only Le Saux became universally known under his Indian name. Unlike Monchanin, he surrendered to a Hindu guru, and was at home in the pilgrimage sites, the maths and ashrams of India, mixing freely with swamis and sadhus (renunciates) the length and breadth of the subcontinent. One also gets the impression, in reading the writings of the two men (including their more intimate letters and journals), that Abhishiktananda suffers little of Monchanin's angst about their missionizing. Indeed, he affirms quite explicitly that the true monk has no essential function but to *be*. In a tribute to Monchanin he wrote that

> The monk is a man who lives in the solitude (Greek: monos) of God, alone in the very aloneness of the Alone.... He does not become a monk in order to do social work or intellectual work or missionary work or to save the world. The monk simply consecrates himself to God.[1]

Abhishiktananda makes an interesting contrast with Monchanin insofar as he *gave primacy to his own mystical realization* over the theological doctrines to which he was formally committed as a Christian. As he somewhere remarked, 'Truth has to be taken from wherever it comes; that Truth possesses us—we do not possess Truth.' On the basis of his own testimony and that of those who knew him in later years we can say of Abhishiktananda that, through the penetration of religious forms, he became a fully realized *sannyasi*—which is to say, neither Hindu nor Christian, or, if one prefers, both Christian and Hindu, this only being possible at a mystical level where the relative forms are universalized. As he wrote in *The Further Shore*, 'The call to

---

1. Abhishiktananda, *The Further Shore* (New Delhi: ISPCK, 1975), p13.

complete renunciation cuts across all dharmas and disregards all frontiers ... it is anterior to every religious formulation.'[1] One of his disciples referred to his 'glorious transfiguration' and 'the transparence of his whole being to the inner Mystery, the divine Presence'.[2] (The fact that this kind of language is used indiscriminately about all manner of dubious 'gurus' should not blind us to the fact that, in some cases—and this is one—such language is perfectly appropriate.) In his diary he wrote of himself as 'at once so deeply Christian and so deeply Hindu, at a depth where Christian and Hindu in their social and mental structures are blown to pieces, and are yet found again ineffably at the heart of each other'.[3] As Frithjof Schuon reminds us,

> When a man seeks to escape from 'dogmatic narrowness' it is essential that it should be 'upwards' and not 'downwards': dogmatic form is transcended by fathoming its depths and contemplating its universal content, and not by denying it in the name of a pretentious and iconoclastic 'ideal' of 'pure truth'.[4]

Abhishiktananda never denied or repudiated the doctrines or practices of either Christianity or Hinduism, nor did he cease to observe the Christian forms of worship and to celebrate the sacraments; rather, he came to understand their limitations as religious *forms*, a form necessarily being limited by definition. His own 'statements' on doctrinal matters, he said, were to be regarded as 'no more than working hypotheses' and as 'vectors of free inquiry.'[5] Religious structures (doctrines, rituals, laws, techniques etc.) were *signposts* to the Absolute but could not be invested with any absolute value themselves.[6] In this insight he again echoes Schuon who writes:

1. Ibid., p27.
2. O. Baumer-Despeigne, 'The Spiritual Journey of Henri Le Saux', p327.
3. J.M.D. Stuart, 'Sri Ramana Maharshi and Abhishiktananda', p173.
4. F. Schuon, *Stations of Wisdom* (London: Perennial Books, 1961), p16.
5. O. Baumer-Despeigne, op. cit., p320.
6. Abhishiktananda, *The Secret of Arunachala* (New Delhi: ISPCK, 1978), p47.

Exotericism consists in identifying transcendent realities with the dogmatic forms, and if need be, with the historical facts of a given Revelation, whereas esotericism refers in a more or less direct manner to these same realities.[1]

It is true that Abhishiktananda many times referred to the tensions arising out of the simultaneous 'presence of the *Upanishads* and the Gospel in a single heart'[2] and that he occasionally used the language of fulfilment when addressing Christians but this would seem to have been a case of *upaya*, 'skilful means' as the Buddhists have it, or what Schuon calls 'saving mirages'.[3] As Schuon also observes, 'In religious exoterisms, efficacy at times takes the place of truth, and rightly so, given the nature of the men to whom they are addressed.'[4] In Abhishiktananda's case we can trace through his writings a move *away* from all notions of Christian exclusivism and triumphalism, *towards* the *sophia perennis*. All the evidence suggests that Abhishiktananda did indeed undergo the plenary experience and see that Light that, in Koranic terms, is 'neither of the East nor of the West.' In communicating that experience, and the knowledge that it delivers, Abhishiktananda felt comfortable resorting to the spiritual vocabulary of both theistic Christianity and monistic Vedanta. Take, for instance, passages such as these:

> The knowledge (*vidya*) of Christ is identical with what the Upanishads call divine knowledge (*brahmavidya*).... It comprises the whole of God's self-manifestation in time, and is one with his eternal self-manifestation.[5]

> Step by step I descended into what seemed to me to be successive depths of my true self—my being (*sat*), my aware-

1. F. Schuon, *Logic and Transcendence* (New York: Harper & Row, 1975), p144.

2. O. Baumer-Despeigne, 'The Spiritual Journey of Henri Le Saux', p310.

3. F. Schuon, *Survey of Metaphysics and Esoterism* (Bloomington: World Wisdom, 1986), p185, n2.

4. F. Schuon, *The Transfiguration of Man* (Bloomington: World Wisdom, 1995), p8.

5. Abhishiktananda, *Guru and Disciple* (London: SPCK, 1974), pxi.

ness of being (*cit*), and my joy in being (*ananda*). Finally nothing was left but he himself, the Only One, infinitely alone, Being, Awareness and Bliss, *Saccidananda.*[1]

In his Introduction to the English edition of *Saccidananda*, Abhishiktananda states:

> Dialogue may begin simply with relations of mutual sympathy. It only becomes worthwhile when it is accompanied by full openness...not merely at the intellectual level, but with regard to [the] inner life of the Spirit. Dialogue about doctrines will be more fruitful when it is rooted in a real spiritual experience at depth and when each one understands that diversity does not mean disunity, once the Centre of all has been reached.[2]

One measure of Abhishiktananda's mystical extinction in Advaitic non-dualism, and the problems this posed for some of his Christian contemporaries (and for all rigidly theistic theologies), is evident in a talk he prepared in the last months of his life:

> In this annihilating experience [of Advaita] one is no longer able to project in front of oneself anything whatsoever, to recognize any other 'pole' to which to refer oneself and to give the name of God. Once one has reached that innermost center, one is so forcibly seized by the mystery that one can no longer utter a 'Thou' or an 'I'. Engulfed in the abyss, we disappear to our own eyes, to our own consciousness. The proximity of that mystery which the prophetic traditions name 'God' burns us so completely that there is no longer any question of discovering it in the depths of oneself or oneself in the depths of it. In the very engulfing, the gulf has vanished. If a cry was still possible—at the moment perhaps of disappearing into the abyss—it would be paradoxically: 'but there is no abyss, no gulf, no distance!'

1. Abhishiktananda, *Saccidananda: A Christian Experience of Advaita* (New Delhi: ISPCK, 1984), p172.

2. Ibid., p xiii.

There is no face-to-face, for there is only That-Which-Is, and no other to name it.[1]

This passage, reminiscent of Eckhart, can take its place amongst the most exalted of mystical commentaries; it also dispels any doubts as to the validity and fullness of Abhishiktananda's own mystical annihilation, called by whatever name.

The last decade of Abhishiktananda's life saw the publication of a series of books bearing the fragrance of his long years of prayer, meditation, study and spiritual awakening. The English-language versions of these books are: *The Mountain of the Lord* (1966), an account of his pilgrimage to Gangotri, the sacred source of the Ganges, *Prayer* (1967), *Hindu-Christian Meeting Point* (1969), *The Church in India* (1969), *Towards the Renewal of the Indian Church* (1970), *Saccidananda: A Christian Experience of Advaita* (1974), *Guru and Disciple* (1974), and *The Secret of Arunachala* (1974), in which he recalls his experiences with Ramana and with Gnanananda, and *The Further Shore* (1975), his deepest meditation on *the Upanishads* and the ideal of *sannyasa*. A collection of several of his essays appeared posthumously as *The Eyes of Light* (1979).

There can be no doubt that, in the words of his friend Raimundo Pannikar, Abhishiktananda was 'one of the most authentic witnesses of our times of the encounter in depth between Christian and Eastern spiritualities.'[2] But his significance goes well beyond this. In his last work, *The Further Shore*, Abhishiktananda writes movingly and wisely of the ideal of the *sannyasi*:

Sannyasa confronts us with a sign of that which is essentially beyond all signs—indeed, in its sheer transparency [to the Absolute] it proclaims its own death as a sign.... However the *sannyasi* lives in the world of signs, of the divine manifestation, and this world of manifestation needs him, 'the

---

1. W. Teasdale, 'Bede Griffiths as Visionary Guide' in *The Other Half of My Soul: Bede Griffiths and Hindu-Christian Dialogue*, ed. B. Bruteau, (Wheaton: Quest, 1994), p14.
2. J.E. Royster, 'Abhishiktananda: Hindu-Christian Monk', p308.

one beyond signs', so that it may realize the impossible possibility of a bridge between the two worlds.... The sign of
sannyasa ... stands then on the very frontier, the unattain-
able frontier. Between two worlds, the world of manifestation and the world of the unmanifest Absolute. It is the
mystery of the sacred lived with the greatest possible interi-
ority. It is a powerful means of grace—that grace which is
nothing else than the Presence of the Absolute, the Eternal,
the Unborn, existing at the heart of the realm of becoming,
of time, of death and life; and a grace which is at the same
time the irresistible drawing of the entire universe and its
fullness towards the ultimate fullness of the Awakening to
the Absolute, to the *Atman*.... Finally, it is even the *taraka*,
the actual one who himself carries men across to the other
shore, the one and only 'ferryman', manifested in manifold
ways in the form of all those rishis, mahatmas, gurus and
buddhas, who throughout history have themselves been
woken and in turn awaken their brother-men.[1]

Abhishiktananda himself came to embody and to live this
ideal. No man could have a more sublime epitaph.

1. Abhishiktananda, *The Further Shore*, pp 42–43.

Frithjof Schuon,
A Sage for the Times

The remembrance of God is our true homeland....[1]
Frithjof Schuon

Portrait

Frithjof Schuon was born in Basle, in 1907, the second son of German parents. His father, Paul Schuon, was an accomplished concert violinist and a professor at the Basle Conservatory of Music. The Schuon brothers were raised in an atmosphere redolent with medievalism, German romanticism and Lutheran piety. Late in life Frithjof Schuon recalled this ambience, 'nurtured by the Middle Ages, at once chivalrous, enchanted and mystical....'[2] Erich, the elder brother, became a Trappist monk and spent most of his life in the Abbaye Notre Dame de Scourmont in Belgium. He developed an intimate relationship with the Oglala holy man Black Elk and was adopted into the Lakota tribe. Frithjof was schooled in both French and German but left school at sixteen to work as a textile designer in Paris.

Even as a young schoolboy Schuon evinced a deep spirituality. By the age of ten he was reading Plato. From an early age he devoted himself to a study of philosophy, religion, and metaphysics, reading the classical and modern works of European philosophy and the sacred literatures of the East. Amongst the Western sources Plato and Eckhart left a profound impression while the *Bhagavad Gita* was his favorite Eastern

1. Letter to Leo Schaya, March 1983, quoted in J-B. Aymard & P. Laude, *Frithjof Schuon: Life and Teachings* (Albany: SUNY, 2004), p27.
2. J-B. Aymard & P. Laude, op. cit., p7.

reading.[1] Of Schuon's youthful writings, one of his biographers has remarked,

> His own discourse was rather of a mystical nature and in his intimate diary one sees a great melancholy, a feeling of irrepressible solitude, a nostalgia for the Eternal Feminine, an unutterable aspiration toward the Beautiful and the Sovereign Good.[2]

After the death of his beloved father in 1920, and a period of intense suffering, Schuon entered the fold of the Catholic Church. In his unpublished *Memoirs* he writes,

> In Catholicism I loved the liturgical manifestation of the holy, the beauty of the divine service in the Gothic-style churches, the cult of Mary and the Rosary; but I could not stop with this, for I had early read the *Bhagavad-Gita* and profoundly experienced the sacred art of the Far East.[3]

He felt at home in this religious milieu but later became increasingly frustrated and alienated by ecclesiastical narrow-mindedness and by the rigid exclusivism which tyrannized the Latin Church. Even after his formal commitment to Islam he retained a mystical affinity for both Christ and His Mother, in 1965 experiencing the overwhelming presence of the Blessed Virgin.[4]

In 1924 Schuon came into contact with the writings of René Guénon, 'which served to confirm his own intellectual rejection of the modern civilisation while at the same time bringing into sharper focus his spontaneous understanding of metaphysical principles and their traditional applications.'[5] He had for several

1. B. Perry, *Frithjof Schuon, Metaphysician and Artist* (Bloomington: World Wisdom, 1981), p 2.

2. J-B. Aymard & P. Laude, op. cit., p 11.

3. Unpublished *Memoirs*, per Michael Fitzgerald.

4. On these experiences and Schuon's veneration of the Virgin see J-B. Aymard & P. Laude, op. cit., pp 41–42.

5. B. Perry, ibid., p 2. See also W. Perry, 'The Revival of Interest in Tradition' in *The Unanimous Tradition*, ed. R. Fernando (Colombo: Sri Lanka Institute of Traditional Studies, 1991), pp 14–16.

years immersed himself in the texts of the Vedanta as well as other Eastern scriptures, finding therein the metaphysical wisdom to which he was thenceforth to devote his life. He felt a particular affinity to both the Hindu tradition and to Taoism. From his earliest years Schuon was also fascinated by traditional art, especially that of Japan and the Far East. In an unusual personal reference in one of his works he tells us of a Buddha figure in an ethnographical museum. It was a traditional representation in gilded wood and flanked by two statues of the Bodhisattvas Seishi and Kwannon. The encounter with this 'overwhelming embodiment of an infinite victory of the Spirit' Schuon sums up in the phrase *'veni, vidi, victus sum'*.[1] One commentator has drawn attention to the importance of aesthetic intuition in accounting for Schuon's extraordinary understanding of traditional religious and social forms:

> It suffices for him to see...an object from a traditional civilisation, to be able to perceive, through a sort of 'chain-reaction', a whole ensemble of intellectual, spiritual, and psychological ideas.[2]

This may seem an extravagant claim but those who have read Schuon's work will not doubt it for a moment. Nor is it any surprise that Schuon was himself a distinguished painter, drawing his themes and subjects from the spiritual traditions of both East and West and that of the American Indians, and from his own mystical visions.

After working for a time in Mulhouse, in Alsace, Schuon underwent a year and a half of military service before returning to his design work in Paris. There, in 1930, his interest in Islam led him to a close study of Arabic, first with a Syrian Jew and afterwards at the Paris mosque.[3] About his own spiritual trajectory he later wrote,

---

1. F. Schuon, *In the Tracks of Buddhism* (London: Allen & Unwin), p121. See also B. Perry, *Frithjof Schuon, Metaphysician and Artist*, p2.
   2. B. Perry, op. cit., p1.
   3. Ibid., p3.

Being *a priori* a metaphysician, I have had since my youth a particular interest in *Advaita Vedanta*, but also in the spiritual method of realization of which *Advaita Vedanta* approves. Since I could not find this method—in its strict and esoteric form—in Europe, and since it was impossible for me to turn to a Hindu guru because of the laws of the castes, I had to look elsewhere.... I finally decided to look for a Sufi master; the outer form did not matter to me.[1]

After a series of providential signs, in 1932 Schuon found himself in Mostaghanem in Algeria, at the feet of Shaykh Ahmad Al'Alawi, the Sufi sage and founder of the 'Alawi order.[2] Schuon has written of this modern saint as

someone who represents in himself... the idea which for hundreds of years has been the life-blood of that civilisation [the Islamic]. To meet such a one is like coming face to face, in mid-twentieth century, with a medieval Saint or a Semitic Patriarch.[3]

Early in 1933 Schuon was formally initiated as a Sufi and given the name Isa Nur ad-Din ('Light of the tradition/s'). Late in 1936 a series of deep experiences revealed to Schuon his role as a spiritual guide; in 1935 he became a *muqaddam* and in 1938 was invested as *shaykh*. Although he never proselytized, from this time on he fulfilled the role of a spiritual master, and various spiritual communities grew up under his leadership. Although his teachings were universal and esoteric, and although he accepted disciples from different traditions, he always insisted that his followers belong to an orthodox religious tradition within which they could observe the essential rites and obligations.

1. Unpublished writings, per Michael Fitzgerald.

2. On the Shaykh see M. Lings, *A Sufi Saint of the Twentieth Century* (Berkeley: University of California, 1971). There is a moving portrait of the Shaykh by Schuon, facing page 160. See also M. Valsan, 'Notes on the Shaikh al-'Alawi, 1869–1934', *Studies in Comparative Religion*, 5:1, 1971.

3. F. Schuon, 'Rahimahu Llah', *Cahiers du Sud*, Aug-Sept 1935, quoted in M. Lings, *A Sufi Saint*, p116.

In the years before the war Schuon several times visited North Africa, sometimes in the company of his school days friend, Titus Burckhardt, spending time in Algeria, Morocco and Egypt where he met René Guénon, with whom he had been corresponding for some years. In many respects Schuon's work was to be an elaboration of principles first given public expression by Guénon. It was in these years that Schuon launched his public writings as an expositor of metaphysical doctrines and of religious forms.

The contemplative climate of India also exercised a strong attraction but a visit to the subcontinent was cut short by the outbreak of World War II which obliged Schuon to return to Europe. He served for some months in the French army before being captured by the Germans. His father had been a native of southern Germany while his mother had come from German-Alsatian stock. Such a background ensured some measure of freedom for Schuon but when the Nazis threatened to forcibly enlist Alsatians in the German army he seized an opportunity to escape across the rugged Jura Mountains into Switzerland. He was detained by the Swiss military until he could verify that he had been born in Basle. He settled in Lausanne and, some years later, took out Swiss nationality.[1]

Two of the most profound books of the century—indeed one could argue that they remain unsurpassed as books which unravel some of the darkest enigmas of our times—appeared within a few years of each other. The first, in 1945, was René Guénon's *magnum opus*, the culmination of his lifework as a writer, *The Reign of Quantity*; the second, appearing meteor-like in 1948, was *The Transcendent Unity of Religions*, Schuon's first major work in which he spells out the metaphysical foundations of the *religio perennis*, that timeless wisdom which informs all integral religious traditions. It is worth noting that Schuon's book made clear several divergences between Guénon and himself, particularly concerning Christian esoterism and the efficacy of the sacraments. It was perfectly apparent that whatever

1. B. Perry, op. cit., p3.

debts Schuon owed to the elderly French metaphysician, with whom he remained on cordial terms despite some strenuous disagreements, he had attained full intellectual independence. It was also now evident that Schuon was embarking on an intellectual program even more far-reaching than that of Guénon, namely, not only the exposition of metaphysical and cosmological doctrines but, in the light of those timeless principles which Guénon had so forcefully elaborated, the penetration of religious forms and sacred art from around the globe and from all the major religious and sapiential traditions.

In 1949 Schuon married Catherine Feer, the daughter of a Swiss diplomat. It was his wife who introduced him to the beauties of the Swiss Alps. Schuon's love of nature, which runs through his work like a haunting melody, was further deepened during two periods which he and his wife spent with the Plains Indians of North America. 'For Schuon, virgin nature carries a message of eternal truth and primordial reality, and to plunge oneself therein is to rediscover a dimension of the soul which in modern man has become atrophied.'[1] Schuon himself, writing in the context of Red Indian receptivity to the lessons of nature, said this:

> Wild Nature is at one with holy poverty and also with spiritual childlikeness; she is an open book containing an inexhaustible teaching of truth and beauty. It is in the midst of his own artifices that man most easily becomes corrupted, it is they who make him covetous and impious; close to virgin Nature, who knows neither agitation nor falsehood, he had the hope of remaining contemplative like Nature herself.[2]

Schuon and his wife had previously developed friendly contacts with visiting Indians in Paris and Brussels in the 1950s. During their first visit to North America in 1959, the Schuons were officially adopted into the Red Cloud family of the Lakota tribe, that branch of the Sioux nation from which came the revered

1. Ibid., p6.
2. F. Schuon, *Light on the Ancient Worlds* (London: Perennial Books, 1966), p84.

'medicine-man' Black Elk.[1] Schuon, Coomaraswamy, and Joseph Epes Brown were all instrumental in efforts to preserve the precious spiritual heritage of the Plains Indians.[2]

During the forty years he lived in Switzerland Schuon travelled in North Africa, the Middle East, and the United States, maintaining close friendships with representatives of all the great religious traditions. Amongst those whom he counted as close personal friends were the perennialists Titus Burckhardt, Leo Schaya, and Whitall Perry, and the American Indian, Chief Thomas Yellowtail of the Crow. Seyyed Hossein Nasr and Martin Lings were amongst his best-known Islamic disciples, each to make their own distinctive contribution to the emergence of the traditionalist 'school'. Of the many distinguished scholars, teachers and spiritual leaders with whom Schuon came into contact we may mention the Russian Archimandrite and later Archbishop Anthony Bloom, Staretz Sophrony of Athos, Father Thomas Merton, Inayat Khan, Shaykh Hassan of Morocco, the renowned Hindu saint Swami Ramdas, Zen Buddhist priests and masters such as Shojun Bando, Sohaku Ogata, and Shinichi Hismatsu, the Tibetan teacher Lobsang Lhalungpa, and Marco Pallis, who was often to act as Schuon's emissary in the East. Schuon also had a special relationship with the Jagadguru of Kanchipuram, the living representative of the spiritual tradition that stretches back through sixty-eight generations to the great Vedantin sage Sankara. Schuon also experienced several intense dreams and visions in which he encountered such figures as Ramakrishna and Ramana Maharshi, two of the most radiant saints and sages of the recent Hindu tradition.

Two spiritual methods became increasingly important to Schuon during the Swiss years, and he continued to advocate them until his death: the *dhikr* (Remembrance of God), also

---

1. For some account of the Schuons' personal experiences with the Plains Indians see F. Schuon, *The Feathered Sun* (Bloomington: World Wisdom, 1990), Parts 2 & 3, and J-B. Aymard & P. Laude, op. cit.

2. See R. Lipsey, *Coomaraswamy: His Life and Work* (Princeton: Princeton University, 1977), pp227–228.

known as the 'invocation', or 'prayer of the heart'; and the *khal-wah* (retreat).[1] These methods were perfectly in accord with the quintessential esoterism which he explicated in his writings but were not always clearly understood by others, even with the *tarîqah*.

Schuon moved to the United States in 1980, making his home in Bloomington, Indiana. He devoted his later years to his volu-minous metaphysical writings and poetry, and to the guidance of the *tarîqah* of which he was the Shaykh. He departed this life in 1998. The funeral ceremony included the recitation of a cou-plet he wrote shortly before his passing:

> *Because I made my heart a holy shrine,*
> *My soul belongs to God, and God is mine.*

His tomb, attended by deer, is in the lovely woods in which he had walked and meditated daily.

Schuon's daily life, governed by a rigorous spiritual discipline, remained much the same throughout his adult years. His wife Catherine has afforded us some glimpses of his daily routines in Lausanne, and by so doing reveals something of his tempera-ment and disposition:

[Frithjof Schuon] was leading a highly disciplined life, punctuated by times of prayer; ever hard on himself, he was on the contrary indulgent with his disciples, taking into account the difficult work conditions of the modern world. He never changed his habits during all the years we lived together. He would get up at dawn and perform his prayers. 'As long as one has not said one's prayers, one is not a human being.' After a simple breakfast, he would walk down to the lake alone.... He had a strict need for these hours of solitude outdoors. At ten o'clock he would receive visitors and in the afternoon, after having retired for an hour, he would write articles or letters. He answered all his mail with admirable patience and generosity.... Often he

1. See J-B. Aymard & P. Laude, op. cit., p27.

would write until late at night and would get up and go back and forth in his room, less to ponder what he wished to express than to remember God. Every day he would read one page in the *Qu'ran* (in Arabic) and he also loved to read the Psalms—Psalms 23, 63, 77, and 124 were his favorites.

We would eat sitting either on the floor or at a small Moroccan table or in the kitchen, in silence. 'One should respect the food'.... When seated, he would never lean back.... He would always walk in a straight, upright fashion, even during the last months of his life.... He would wash only with cold water; to take a hot bath occurred to him as little as to smoke a hookah! If it is true that some of his habits stemmed from the fact that we had always been poor, they correspond on the other hand to his ascetic nature. Everything he did, he would do well, without hurry, with recollected mien.[1]

In *The Conference of the Birds*, the great Sufi mystic, Farid Ud-Din Attar, enjoins the spiritual seeker to 'Put on the mantle of nothingness.' Schuon covered his own life with the cloak of anonymity, maintaining a deliberate obscurity and detachment from public affairs. Like his predecessor René Guénon, Schuon had no interest in noisy acclaim, nor was he in any sense the worldy 'intellectual'—quite the contrary. In one of his early books he remarked that 'the more serious among [Eastern] spiritual teachers'

are showing an increasing tendency to withdraw themselves as far as possible from the public gaze in order that the wisdom they have to impart may become sufficiently hard of access to filter out, as it were, the unqualified, leaving the door open to those only who, guided thither by the divine Grace, are prepared to pay the proper price.[2]

---

1. C. Schuon, 'Frithjof Schuon: Memories and Anecdotes', *Sacred Web*, 8, 2001, pp53–54.
2. F. Schuon, *Language of the Self* (Madras: Ganesh, 1959), p50.

This seems to have been the posture that Schuon himself adopted, one not excluding friendly relations with other spiritual teachers and representatives of the different traditions.

It would be quite impertinent for an outsider, such as the present author, to mount any 'assessment' of Schuon's role as a spiritual guide: only those blessed to be his disciples, in some more or less direct sense, are in a position to understand and comment on Schuon's spiritual function. Readers interested in this facet of Schuon's life are directed to the several sources which have become available since his passing.[1] Here we will restrict ourselves to a few remarks about some of the confusion, obfuscation and discord which in recent years has accumulated around the person and the role Frithjof Schuon, leaving aside the inevitable incomprehensions and hostilities of those who are quite incapable of understanding even the simplest messages of Tradition, let alone grasping the esoteric wisdom which Schuon was ever expressing anew. However, various tensions, controversies, and polemical eruptions have arisen within the 'traditionalist' or 'perennialist' movement itself, calling for some comment.

Some of the forces at work here include over-zealous and misguided attempts to isolate René Guénon as the exclusive master of metaphysics in our time, and the final arbiter on all matters pertaining to tradition; the 'passional blindness' and pious extravagances of some representatives of religious orthodoxy who believed, wrongly, that Schuon had compromised the integrity of religious forms; and the squalid calumnies leveled at this noble soul by some lost individuals under the sway of a malevolence which thinks nothing of defiling the reputations of the most saintly of men and women. Jean-Baptiste Aymard, one of Schuon's biographers, reminds us of analogous cases involving no less than St Teresa of Ávila, Padre Pio, and Ramana

---

1. See J-B. Aymard & P. Laude, op. cit.; M. Fitzgerald, 'Frithjof Schuon: Providence without Paradox', *Sacred Web*, 8, 2001; and R. Fabbri, 'Naked Truth: The Prophet, the Saint and the Sage', *Sacred Web*, 20, 2007.

Maharshi. He also cites Schiller's sombre observation that 'the world seeks to blacken what shines and to drag into the dust what is sublime.'[1] In Aymard and Laude's biography each of these groups critical of Schuon is quietly disarmed through a sober consideration of the facts of Schuon's relationship to Guénon (many of which have not previously come to light in published form), and through an explanation of the somewhat different roles that each providentially fulfilled; through a careful and persuasive explication of Schuon's stance in regard to religious forms; and through an affirmation of those qualities which made Schuon quite incapable of the offences with which his detractors had vilified him.

All of Schuon's work, particularly his more intimate and later writings, are shot through with references to prayer. In a rare interview in 1996, when asked about his message for people in general, he replied,

> Prayer. To be a human means to be connected with God. Life has no meaning without this. Prayer, and also beauty, of course; for we live among forms and not in a cloud. Beauty of soul first and then beauty of symbols around us.[2]

It seems appropriate, then, to end our overview of Schuon's life with a poignant passage from one of his earliest books in which his sense of prayer and his love of the beauty of natural forms converge.

> Man prays and prayer fashions man. The saint has himself become prayer, the meeting place of earth and Heaven; and thereby he contains the universe and the universe prays with him. He is everywhere where nature prays and he prays with her and in her: in the peaks which touch the void and eternity, in a flower which scatters its scent or in

1. J-B. Aymard & P. Laude, op. cit., p51.
2. D. Casey, 'The Basis of Religion and Metaphysics: An Interview with Frithjof Schuon', *The Quest*, Summer 1996, pp77–78.

the carefree song of a bird. He who lives in prayer has not lived in vain.[1]

A fitting epitaph.

Oeuvre

Before I turn to a conspectus of Schuon's writings I hope the reader will allow a brief reminiscence which may strike a chord. Some thirty-odd years ago, browsing through a magazine in rather desultory fashion, my eye caught a review of *The Sword of Gnosis*, an anthology of writings on 'Metaphysics, Cosmology, Tradition, Symbolism', edited by Jacob Needleman. The review was sufficiently arresting for me to seek out a copy of the book. It was with growing excitement that I first encountered the writings of several figures whose work I would come to know well over the years ahead—René Guénon, Titus Burckhardt, Martin Lings, Marco Pallis, Seyyed Hossein Nasr, amongst others. But the effect of Frithjof Schuon's several essays in this anthology was quite mesmeric: here, in the exposition of traditional doctrines and principles, was a clarity, a radiance, and a depth which seemed to me, as indeed it still does, to be of a more or less miraculous order. Nasr has written of the appearance of Guénon's first book (*Introduction générale à l'étude des doctrines des hindoues*, 1921),

> It was like a sudden burst of lightning, an abrupt intrusion into the modern world of a body of knowledge and a perspective utterly alien to the prevalent climate and world view and completely opposed to all that characterizes the modern mentality.[2]

This, precisely, is how Schuon's essays struck me. My own intellectual and spiritual life was changed forever. At that time, Schuon's books were not easily available in Australia. It was in

1. F. Schuon, *Spiritual Perspectives and Human Facts* (London: Perennial Books, 1967), p223.
2. S.H. Nasr, *Knowledge and the Sacred* (New York: Crossroad, 1981), p101.

the face of some difficulties that I rapidly accumulated not only Schuon's works but those of other contemporary exponents of the *sophia perennis*. I soon felt the force of Ananda Coomaraswamy's remark that

> if you ever really enter into this other world, you may not wish to return: you may never again be content with what you have been accustomed to think of as 'progress' and 'civilization'.[1]

*

Schuon's published work forms an imposing corpus and covers a staggering range of religious and metaphysical subjects without any of the superficialities and simplifications which we normally expect from someone covering such a vast terrain. His works on specific religious traditions have commanded respect from leading scholars and practitioners within the traditions in question. As well as publishing more than thirty books he was a prolific contributor to journals such as *Études Traditionnelles*, *Islamic Quarterly*, *Tomorrow*, *Studies in Comparative Religion*, and *Sophia Perennis*. All his major works, written in French, have now been published in English. Since his death his vast poetic output, as well as some of his correspondence, has appeared in English translation.

Schuon's works are all governed by an unchanging set of metaphysical principles. They exhibit nothing of a 'development' or 'evolution' but are, rather, re-statements of the same principles from different vantage points and brought to bear on divergent phenomena. Schuon's vision was complete from the outset. Nor is the term 'erudition' quite appropriate: Schuon not only knows 'about' an encyclopedic range of religious manifestations and sapiential traditions but seems to understand them in a way which, for want of a better word, we can only call intuitive. His writings in this field are without equal.

1. A. Coomaraswamy, 'Medieval and Oriental Art', in *Coomaraswamy 1: Selected Papers, Traditional Art and Symbolism* (Princeton: Princeton University Press, 1977), pp 45–46.

All of Schuon's work is concerned with a re-affirmation of traditional metaphysical principles, with an explication of the esoteric dimensions of religion, with the penetration of mythological and religious forms, and with the critique of a modernism which is either indifferent or nakedly hostile to the principles which inform all traditional wisdoms. Perennialists are, by definition, committed to expounding the *sophia perennis* which lies at the heart of the diverse religions and within their manifold forms. Schuon's general position—or better, the position to which Schuon adhered, for 'truth is not and cannot be a personal affair'[1]—was defined in his first work to appear in English, *The Transcendent Unity of Religions* (1953), a work of which T.S. Eliot remarked, 'I have met with no more impressive work on the comparative study of Oriental and Occidental religion.'[2] In peerless fashion this book elaborated the distinction between the exoteric and esoteric dimensions of religious traditions and, by uncovering the metaphysical convergence of all orthodox religions, provided a coherent and irrefutable basis for a properly constituted religious ecumenicism—one might well say the *only* possible basis.

Much of Schuon's work has been explicitly directed to the Islamic tradition to which he has devoted four books: *Understanding Islam* (1963); *Dimensions of Islam* (1969); *Islam and the Perennial Philosophy* (1976); and *Sufism: Veil and Quintessence* (1981).[3] Both *Christianity/Islam: Essays on Ecumenic Esotericism* (1985) and *In the*

1. F. Schuon, *Light on the Ancient Worlds*, p 34

2. Quoted by Huston Smith, Introduction to *The Transcendent Unity of Religions* (New York: Harper & Row, 1975, rev. ed.), p ix.

3. In regard to two of these books Michael Fitzgerald has provided the following notes: 'In accordance with Schuon's preference we have not listed either *Dimensions of Islam* or *Islam and the Perennial Philosophy* in the list of his English language compilations. He wrote, "My doctrinal message is in my French books and their translations. It is only indirectly and imperfectly in the English compilations *Dimensions of Islam* and *Islam and the Perennial Philosophy*, which were produced for contingent reasons and do not correspond to my intentions." (Unpublished document...) Many of the chapters in *Dimensions of Islam* are included in the book entitled *Form and Substance in the Religions*, which has been posthumously published for the first time in English [in 2002].'

Face of the Absolute (1989) focus on the Christian and Islamic traditions. Seyyed Hossein Nasr, himself an eminent Islamicist, wrote
of *Understanding Islam*, 'I believe his work to be the most out-
standing ever written in a European language on why Muslims
believe in Islam and why Islam offers to man all that he needs
religiously and spiritually.'[1] Nasr has been no less generous in
commending later works.

Whilst all of Schuon's works have a Sufic fragrance his work
has by no means been restricted to the Islamic heritage. Two
major works focus on Hinduism and Buddhism: *Language of the
Self* (1959) and *In the Tracks of Buddhism* (1969) (a revised and
enlarged version of the latter was published by World Wisdom
Books in 1993 as *Treasures of Buddhism*). It is worth noting that
although Schuon's religious allegiances were to Islam, his intellectuality found its deepest inspiration in Advaita Vedanta, particularly in the *Upanishads* and in the teachings of the 8th
century sage Sankara. Although Schuon has not devoted such
sustained attention to other religious and mythological traditions there are countless illuminating references in Schuon's
work to all manner of religious phenomena and doctrines,
drawn from all over the globe.

Spiritual Perspectives and Human Facts (1954) is a collection of
aphoristic essays including studies of Vedanta and sacred art,
and a meditation on the spiritual virtues. My own most conspicuous memory of first reading this book, apart from a sense of its
crystalline beauty, is of Schuon's compelling contrast between
the principles which govern all traditional art and the pompos-
ity, vacuity, and grotesqueness of much that masquerades as 'art'
in the post-medieval world and which has long since ceased to
'exteriorize either transcendent ideas or profound virtues.'[2]
Schuon's writings on art are often embellished with striking epi-
grams. Who could forget one as telling as this:

1. See S.H. Nasr, *Ideals and Realities of Islam* (London: Allen & Unwin, 1966),
p10.
2. F. Schuon, *Spiritual Perspectives and Human Facts*, p36.

When standing before a [medieval] cathedral, a person really feels he is placed at the centre of the world; standing before a church of the Renaissance, Baroque or Rococo periods, he merely feels himself to be in Europe.[1]

Gnosis: Divine Wisdom (1959), *Logic and Transcendence* (1976), and *Esoterism and Principle and as Way* (1981) are largely given over to extended and explicit discussions of metaphysical principles. The first includes a luminous section on the Christian tradition while *Logic and Transcendence* contains Schuon's most explicit refutation of some of the philosophies and ideologies of modernity. His early arraignment of such characteristically modern philosophies of negation and despair as relativism, rationalism, 'concretism', existentialism, and psychologism put us in mind of the sword of discriminating wisdom wielded by the bodhisattva Manjusri! The later parts of the book tend towards its culmination in this passage:

To the question of what are the foremost things a man should do, situated as he is this world of enigmas and fluctuations, the reply must be made that there are four things to be done or four jewels never to be lost sight of: first, he should accept the Truth; second, bear it continually in mind; third, avoid whatever is contrary to Truth and the permanent consciousness of truth; and fourth, accomplish whatever is in conformity therewith.[2]

Schuon suggested some years ago that *Logic and Transcendence* was his most representative and inclusive work.[3] That distinction is perhaps now shared with *Esoterism as Principle and as Way* which includes Schuon's most deliberate explanation of the nature of esoterism, and with *Survey of Metaphysics and Esoterism* (1986) which is a masterly work of metaphysical synthesis.

1. F. Schuon, *The Transcendent Unity of Religions*, p65, note.

2. F. Schuon, *Logic and Transcendence*, pp265–6.

3. Schuon's comment about *Logic and Transcendence* is recorded in Whitall Perry's review in *Studies in Comparative Religion*, 9:4, 1975, p250.

Stations of Wisdom (1961) is directed mainly towards an exploration of certain religious and spiritual modalities but includes 'Orthodoxy and Intellectuality', an essay of paramount importance in understanding the perennialist position espoused by Schuon. *Light on the Ancient Worlds* includes a range of essays on such subjects as the Hellenist-Christian 'dialogue', shamanism, monasticism, and the *religio perennis*.

The last decade of Schuon's life was astonishingly productive, seeing the appearance of *To Have a Center* (1990), *Roots of the Human Condition* (1991), *Echoes of Perennial Wisdom, The Play of Masks* (1992), *The Transfiguration of Man* (1995), and *The Eye of the Heart* (1997). These later writings exhibit a masterly lightness of touch and a style that is increasingly synthetic and poetic. The title chapter of *To Have a Center* furnishes Schuon's only extended statement concerning the literary and artistic 'culture' of the last two hundred years. Other essays in these books cover such subjects as intellection, prayer, integral anthropology, and art. *Echoes of Perennial Wisdom* (1992) is an anthology of epigrammatic passages and apophthegms from many of Schuon's works.

Schuon's effulgent writings on the spiritual treasury of the Plains Indians have been collected, together with reproductions of some of his paintings, in *The Feathered Sun: Plains Indians in Art and Philosophy* (1990). In one sense this is one of Schuon's most 'personal' books, textured as it is with direct references to his own experience. A further token of this aspect of the book is that one cannot imagine any of his predecessors or contemporaries writing anything like it. The book, in both text and image, is also pervaded by the pathos which marks the disappearance of a spiritual economy and a way of life of extraordinary beauty and nobility. There is a peculiar poignancy in the fact that Schuon was adopted into both the Crow and Sioux tribes, remembering their heroic resistance to the encroachments of 'civilisation'. Furthermore, one cannot but see in Schuon himself just those qualities which he extolled in the Indians—'a stoical and combative heroism with a priestly bearing [which] conferred on the Indian of the Plains and Forest a sort of majesty at once aquiline and solar....'[1]

Patrick Laude has noted five 'points of view' from which 'the distinction between the Divine and what lies outside it' might legitimately be envisaged, namely: meta-theistic metaphysics such as we find in Advaita Vedanta or Taoism; a monotheistic theology which emphasizes the 'fundamental hiatus' between God and his Creation, exemplified by Islam and Judaism; the Logocentric outlook pre-eminent in Christianity and in the Avataric perspective of Hinduism; angelolatry and various forms of so-called polytheism in which angels/deities 'essentially represent Divine aspects'; and, lastly, primordial Shamanism, which calls for 'an ecological participation in the supernatural vocation of Nature' and a thorough-going integration of psychic energies and powers into the spiritual life. The plasticity of Schuon's spiritual sensibility (in some respects reminiscent of that of Paramahamsa Ramakrishna) enabled him, according to the exigencies of the moment, to take the viewpoint of each of these perspectives. Further, as Laude observes elsewhere,

> There is no author more categorical than Schuon when the dazzling evidence of principles imposes itself, but there is no one more attentive to the paradoxes, the compensations and the complex play of necessary exceptions. . . .[2]

In the last few years of his life Schuon composed no less than 3,500 short poems in German, in twenty-three collections, adding to a body of poetry written earlier in French and English. Since Schuon's death some nine volumes of his poems have been published, including two large collections in *World Wheel* (2006) and *Songs Without Names* (2006). In these poems, the principles and insights expressed in his other writings find a lyric voice in the most simple and concise form. This long cycle of poems has been compared to Rumi's *Mathnawi* and to the *Psalms* of David, and as William Stoddart has observed,

1. F. Schuon, *The Feathered Sun*, pp39–40.
2. J-B. Aymard & P. Laude, op. cit., p120.

they are an expression of nostalgia, of mankind's longing for, and ultimate satisfaction in, the Lord.... They are an inexhaustible, and ever new purifying fountain—a crystal-line and living expression of the *religio perennis*. They epito-mize truth, beauty, and salvation.[1]

Many of Schuon's paintings are reproduced in *The Feathered Sun* and *Images of Primordial and Mystic Beauty: Paintings by Frithjof Schuon* (1992). His earliest works, in the main, were sketches of the heads of men from different ethnic backgrounds whilst in mid-life he turned his artistic energies towards a magnificent series of canvases depicting the mythology and ceremonial life of the Plains Indians of North America. His favorite subject in his later years was the Virgin, sometimes rendered in a visual style somewhat reminiscent of Hindu art. 'The subjects treated by Schuon', Patrick Laude observes, 'are essentially of two types:

The world of the American Indians envisaged in its sacer-dotal hieratism and heroic dignity, and the world of femi-ninity, from its virginal innocence in the genre of Gauguin to the mysterious inwardness in the icons of the Virgin.[2]

Jean-Baptiste Aymard cautions that

One will understand nothing of Schuon's teachings if one is unaware of the importance for him of the sacred and beau-tiful, and his inclination—as with every 'visual' type, towards anything that manifests Beauty as such. An impor-tant part of his message is the following: in a centrifugal world of mediocrity and ugliness, the contemplation of beauty is a concrete response, a source of interiorization, a door to the True.[3]

Both Schuon's poetry and his visual art alert us to the vital

---

1. W. Stoddart, Introduction to *World Wheel Volumes I–III: Poems by Frithjof Schuon* (Bloomington: World Wisdom, 2006), pp xiv-xv.
2. J-B. Aymard & P. Laude, *Frithjof Schuon: Life and Teachings*, p 117.
3. Ibid., p 52.

role of Beauty. As one of his biographers has suggested, 'If sapiential intelligence is the directing principle of Schuon's work, beauty is its main mode of manifestation and assimilation.'[1] Further, Beauty itself entails three dimensions, each of which can be linked with the Vedantic ternary and each readily apparent in Schuon's life, teaching and handiwork: 'a doctrine of Beauty which pertains to the domain of metaphysical consciousness' (*cit*); 'a methodical and spiritual awareness of the beautiful as a means of grace' (*sat*); 'a creative joy, a dimension of beatitude (*ananda*), which is expressed by his poetical and pictorial productions and by a contemplative receptivity to feminine beauty as a privileged mirror of the Divine.'[2]

In the last few years several thematic anthologies of Schuon's writings have been published, including *René Guénon: Some Observations* (ed., William Stoddart, 2004), *The Fullness of God: Frithjof Schuon on Christianity* (ed., James Cutsinger, 2004), *Prayer Fashions Man: Frithjof Schuon on the Spiritual Life* (ed., James Cutsinger, 2005), and *Art from the Sacred to the Profane, East and West* (ed., Catherine Schuon, 2006).

There is now a burgeoning literature on Schuon's life and work. Readers are directed to the following: *The Essential Writings of Frithjof Schuon* (1986), which includes S.H. Nasr's magisterial introduction; *Religion of the Heart* (1991), a *Festschrift* compiled for Schuon's eightieth birthday, edited by Nasr and William Stoddart; James Cutsinger's *Advice to the Serious Seeker: Meditations on the Teachings of Frithjof Schuon* (1996); the Frithjof Schuon Memorial Issue of *Sophia*, (4:2, 1998); *Frithjof Schuon; Les Dossiers H* (2002), edited by Jean-Baptiste Aymard and Patrick Laude; *Frithjof Schuon: Life and Teachings* (2004) by Jean-Baptiste Aymard and Patrick Laude; and a more intimate forthcoming biography by Michael Fitzgerald, based on his diaries, letters and other personal writings, *Frithjof Schuon, Messenger of the Perennial Philosophy*.

*

1. Ibid., p125
2. Ibid., p108.

In *Understanding Islam* Schuon had this to say about the nature of Sacred Books:

> that is sacred which in the first place is attached to the tran-
> scendent order, secondly possesses the character of abso-
> lute certainty and, thirdly, eludes the comprehension and
> power of investigation of the ordinary human mind.... The
> sacred is the presence of the centre in the periphery, of the
> motionless in the moving; dignity is essentially an expres-
> sion of it, for in dignity too the centre manifests at the exte-
> rior; the heart is revealed in gestures. The sacred
> introduces a quality of the absolute into relativities and
> confers on perishable things a texture of eternity.[1]

Without wishing to make any extravagant claims such as
might conflate Schuon's writings with holy Scriptures, I do not
think it too much to avow that these qualities are everywhere
manifested in his *oeuvre*. The pervasive sense of the sacred, the
love of prayer, of sacred symbols and of 'modes of Divine Presence', the miraculous sensitivity to 'theophanic manifestations'
and 'celestial perfumes', the discernment of the 'metaphysical
transparency of phenomena', the capacity to grasp the 'principial within the manifested', to see 'the vertical ray', to see God
everywhere—these qualities overflow in Schuon's work and
constitute a providential and incomparable gift to an age apparently determined to turn its back on the sacred.[2]

1. F. Schuon, *Understanding Islam* (London: Allen & Unwin, 1976), p48.
2. The quoted phrases are Schuon's and come from fragments of correspondence published in *The Transfiguration of Man* (Bloomington: World Wisdom,
1995), p113.

Acknowledgments

The essays in this volume first appeared in the following books and journals, to whose publishers and editors thanks are due for permission to reproduce them here. Only minor technical and stylistic changes have been made to the originals, apart from the article on Frithjof Schuon which has been expanded.

'René Guénon, Metaphysician' was first published as 'Biographical Sketch', introducing the third English-language edition of René Guénon, *The Reign of Quantity & the Signs of the Times* (Ghent: Sophia Perennis, 1995), pp vi–xxxvii.

'Ananda Coomaraswamy, Art and Metaphysics' was first published as 'Ananda Coomaraswamy', chapter 3 of Kenneth Oldmeadow, *Traditionalism: Religion in the Light of the Perennial Philosophy* (Colombo: Sri Lanka Institute of Traditional Studies, 2000), pp 26–35.

'Rudolf Otto, the East, and Religious Inclusivism' was first published, in part, in Harry Oldmeadow, *Journeys East: 20th Century Western Encounters with Eastern Religious Traditions* (Bloomington: World Wisdom, 2004).

'Mircea Eliade and C.G. Jung: "Priests without Surplices"? was a talk for the Bendigo Jung Society and published as the first of the series *Studies in Western Traditions: Occasional Papers* (Bendigo: Humanities Department, School of Arts, La Trobe University Bendigo, 1995.)

'Allen Ginsberg, A Buddhist Beat' was first published as 'To a Buddhist Beat: Allen Ginsberg on Poetics, Politics and Spirituality', in *Beyond the Divide*, 2:1, Winter 1999, pp 56–67.

'Swami Abhishiktananda, Fr Jules Monchanin, and the Christian-Hindu Encounter' was first published as 'Jules Monchanin, Henri Le Saux/Abhishiktananda and the Hindu-Christian Encounter', in *Australian Religion Studies Review*, 17:2, 2004, pp 98–113.

'Frithjof Schuon, A Sage for the Times' was first published, in a shorter form, as 'A Sage for the Times: the Role and *Oeuvre* of Frithjof Schuon', in *Sophia: The Journal for Traditional Studies*, 4:2, Winter, 1998, pp 56–67.

The Perennial Philosophy: Recommended Reading

Introductory

James Cutsinger, *Advice to the Serious Seeker: Meditations on the Teachings of Frithjof Schuon* (Albany: SUNY, 1996).

Gai Eaton, *King of the Castle: Choice and Responsibility in the Modern World* (London: Bodley Head, 1977).

Ranjit Fernando (ed.), *The Unanimous Tradition* (Colombo: Sri Lanka Institute of Traditional Studies, 1991).

Martin Lings, *Ancient Beliefs and Modern Superstitions* (London: Allen & Unwin, 1980).

Barry McDonald (ed.), *Every Branch in Me: Essays on the Meaning of Man* (Bloomington: World Wisdom, 2002).

Jacob Needleman (ed.), *The Sword of Gnosis* (Baltimore: Penguin Books, 1974).

W. E. [Lord] Northbourne, *Religion in the Modern World* (London: J.M. Dent, 1963; second, revised and enlarged edition, Sophia Perennis reprint, 2001).

Kenneth Oldmeadow, *Traditionalism: Religion in the light of the Perennial Philosophy* (Colombo: Sri Lanka Institute of Traditional Studies, 2000).

Harry Oldmeadow (ed.), *The Betrayal of Tradition: Essays on the Spiritual Crisis of Modernity* (Bloomington: World Wisdom, 2005).

Marco Pallis, *The Way and the Mountain* (Bloomington: World Wisdom Books, 2008).

Whitall Perry, *Challenges to a Secular Society* (Oakton: Foundation of Traditional Studies, 1996).

Frithjof Schuon, *Spiritual Perspectives and Human Facts* (Bloomington: World Wisdom Books, 2007).

—*Echoes of Perennial Wisdom* (Bloomington: World Wisdom Books, 1993).

Philip Sherrard, *The Sacred in Art & Life* (Ipswich: Golgonooza, 1990).

Huston Smith, *Forgotten Truth* (New York: Harper & Row, 1977).
William Stoddart, *Remembering in a World of Forgetting* (Bloomington: World Wisdom Books, 2008).

More Advanced Reading

J-B. Aymard & P. Laude, *Frithjof Schuon: Life and Teachings* (Albany: SUNY, 2004).

Titus Burckhardt, *Mirror of the Intellect* (Cambridge: Quinta Essentia, 1987).

—*The Essential Titus Burckhardt*, ed. W. Stoddart (Bloomington: World Wisdom Books, 2003).

Ananda Coomaraswamy, *Coomaraswamy Selected Papers, Vol. 1, Traditional Art and Symbolism; Vol. 2, Metaphysics*, ed. Roger Lipsey (Princeton: Princeton University Press, 1977).

—*The Bugbear of Literacy* (Bedfont: Perennial Books, 1979).

—*Christian and Oriental Philosophy of Art* (New York: Dover, 1956).

—*The Essential Coomaraswamy*, ed. R.P. Coomaraswamy (Bloomington: World Wisdom Books, 2004).

René Guénon, *The Reign of Quantity & the Signs of the Times* (Hillsdale: Sophia Perennis, 2004).

—*Man and His Becoming According to the Vedanta* (Hillsdale: Sophia Perennis, 2004).

Brian Keeble (ed.), *Every Man an Artist* (Bloomington: World Wisdom Books, 2005).

Seyyed Hossein Nasr, *Knowledge and the Sacred* (New York: Crossroad, 1981).

—*The Essential Seyyed Hossein Nasr*, ed. William Chittick (Bloomington: World Wisdom Books, 2007).

—& K. O'Brien (eds.), *The Essential Sophia* (Bloomington: World Wisdom Books, 2006).

Whitall Perry (ed.), *A Treasury of Traditional Wisdom* (Louisville: Fons Vitae, 2000).

Leo Schaya, *The Universal Meaning of the Kabbalah* (London: Allen & Unwin, 1971).

Frithjof Schuon, *The Transcendent Unity of Religions* (New York: Harper & Row, 1975).

—*Light on the Ancient Worlds* (Bloomington: World Wisdom Books, 2006).

—*Gnosis: Divine Wisdom* (Bloomington: World Wisdom Books, 2006).

—*Logic and Transcendence* (New York: Harper & Row, 1975).

—*Esoterism as Principle and as Way* (London: Perennial Books, 1990).

—*The Essential Writings of Frithjof Schuon*, ed. S.H. Nasr (Bloomington: World Wisdom Books, 2005).

—*Survey of Metaphysics and Esoterism* (Bloomington: World Wisdom Books, 1986).

Reza Shah-Kazemi, *Paths to Transcendence* (Bloomington: World Wisdom Books, 2006.)

Wolfgang Smith, *Cosmos and Transcendence: Breaking Through the Barrier of Scientistic Belief* (San Rafael: Sophia Perennis, 2008).

'A Monk of the West', *Christianity and the Doctrine of Non-Dualism* (Hillsdale: Sophia Perennis, 2004).

Websites

www.latrobe.edu.au/eyeoftheheart
www.religioperennis.org
www.worldwisdom.com
www.fonsvitae.com
www.sophiaperennis.com
www.sacredweb.com
sophiajournal.com

Journals

Sophia: The Journal of Traditional Studies (Oakton, VA).
Sacred Web: A Journal of Tradition and Modernity (Vancouver).
Eye of the Heart (Bendigo).
Vincit Omnia Veritas (USA/France).
Oriens (France).
The Temenos Academy Review (London).

Note on the Author

Dr Harry Oldmeadow is the Coordinator of Philosophy and Religious Studies in the Arts Program at La Trobe University Bendigo, in Victoria, Australia. He has published many books and articles on religious subjects, most recently *A Christian Pilgrim in India: the Spiritual Journey of Swami Abhishiktananda* (2008). He lives with his wife on a small property in Mandurang, south of Bendigo.

Further information at:
http://www.latrobe.edu.au/prs/staff/oldmeadow.html

Made in the USA
Las Vegas, NV
17 November 2024

11973892R00100